AF598819

TURBULENT JOURNEY

TURBULENT JOURNEY

The Jumo Engine, Operation Paperclip, and the American Dream

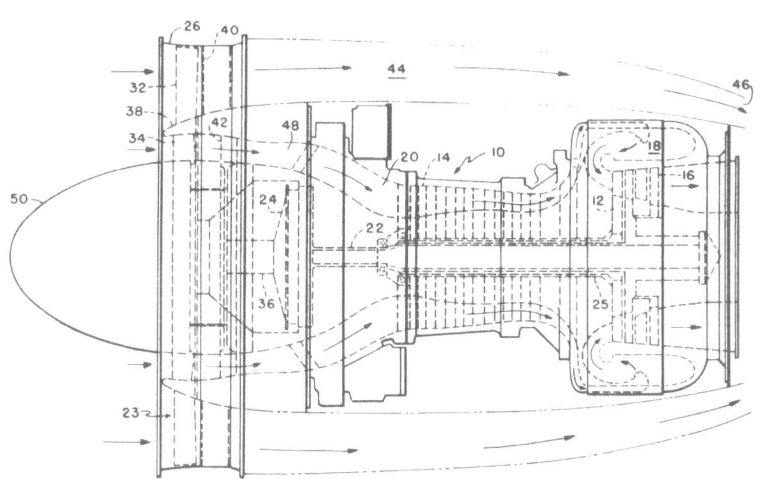

Reiner Decher

Library of Congress Control Number: 2021942584

Designed by Beth Oberholtzer
Cover design by Danielle D. Farmer
Type set in Stolzl/Economica/Crimson/Gotham Narrow

ISBN: 978-0-7643-6355-9
Printed in India

Published by Schiffer Publishing, Ltd.
4880 Lower Valley Road
Atglen, PA 19310
Phone: (610) 593-1777; Fax: (610) 593-2002
Email: Info@schifferbooks.com
Web: www.schifferbooks.com

For our complete selection of fine books on this and related subjects, please visit our website at www.schifferbooks.com. You may also write for a free catalog.

Schiffer Publishing's titles are available at special discounts for bulk purchases for sales promotions or premiums. Special editions, including personalized covers, corporate imprints, and excerpts, can be created in large quantities for special needs. For more information, contact the publisher.

We are always looking for people to write books on new and related subjects. If you have an idea for a book, please contact us at proposals@schifferbooks.com.

To Papa
Who, with strength and wisdom,

And, to Mutti
Who, with kindness and cheer,
Got us through a time like no other
With the help of others and good fortune.

With so much gone right
That could have gone wrong
Where I could have spent
A life behind a curtain
Of Iron and barbed wire.
Could I, would I embrace
the person that I might have been
Being who I am?

CONTENTS

FOREWORD

This is a story of navigating through World War II as a civilian. An engineer's work on a jet engine keeps him from having to fight in the Wehrmacht but does not shield him and his family from the consequences of a losing and lost war. VE-day was not the end of uncertainty and want. Opportunities to leave war-torn Germany and to work on the technology he loves are missed and ultimately realized. Both are consequences of interactions with the US Army. In France, the engineer joins a team that becomes a major jet engine producer in that country. Later, he rejoins his former German colleagues in America, where he is again part of the nucleus of people that started an important American producer of jet engines. In that setting, his work impacted the design and operation of every airliner. The story is told not by the central figure of this tale, but by the son who followed him not only as a child but also in his footsteps. In that sense, I explore the question: How did I get here?

Reiner Decher
Bellevue, Washington
March 2020

ACKNOWLEDGMENTS

The story is based in part on a "Decher Family Book" written by the subject, Siegfried H. Decher. I will refer to him as "Sig," the name he acquired from colleagues during his professional life in the United States. To his family, he was Papa. The family book includes the identification of our various parents and grandparents, where they lived, what they did in life, and life dates. Mention of other more distant relatives and friends who we, the readers, might know or remember also illustrate the book. The readers of Sig's book were meant to be the author of this story, his brother Uli, and their progeny. It was not written with a wider audience in mind.

After Sig died in 1980, I used his files to frame the backbone of this book. They contained personal and business correspondence, along with technical papers and books that he viewed as an important part of his work. Official documents such as educational achievements, identification cards, passports, and the like were carefully documented. This tale is an interpreted transcription of much of what is in these files. Central to that body of work was a notebook containing descriptions and backgrounds on the patents he was awarded. Two of his most important patents are featured here. In addition to the private records, publications that detail his work in connection with the companies that employed him were also a rich trove of details.

Notably absent in what he left is the emotional connectivity that makes a story interesting. That had to be read between the lines and is woven into this retelling, where appropriate and available.

A number of elements of the journey described here are filled by Sig's wife, our mother. After our father died, my brother and I asked her to document her wartime experiences. She wrote down much of what we now know, events that occurred when we were too young to remember. Her contribution of detailed facts and the emotional landscape of the time was greatly appreciated.

Our story is also strengthened by an unpublished life story written by Karsten Eggers. His father, Gerhard Eggers, was an aerodynamicist specializing in engine installation (in airplanes) who worked at Junkers and went to France at the same time as our family. It is with gratitude that I received his story in 2018 and, upon reading it, relived the many details of our common journey through pictures and words. I hereby gratefully acknowledge his contribution to my understanding of these early times and the use of pictures from his memoir.

The photographs without stated credits are the author's, primarily from the files of the subject of our story but also taken at various museums, as noted. A word of thanks is due to the corporate entities noted in the caption credits, for providing images to enrich the story.

A special thanks for our better understanding of the family history and the included maps is due to Sig's great-nephew Andreas Illert. Thanks are also due to the audiences listening to my telling of the salient points of this story. The suggestion that I write this story for posterity was reinforced by Steve Little and other colleagues at the Museum of Flight in Seattle. Very much appreciated are the comments on reading the drafts by my brother-in-law, Charles Bunting, and by Annegret Marchisella, Sig's great-niece. I am especially grateful to my wife, Mary, for her patience and tolerating my wordsmithing on this keyboard and for her corrections, both of which greatly helped this story come to fruition!

A War-Torn Century

An interesting life may be best described by the person who lived it. When the memory is grounded in a desire to put it into a more distant past or forgetting it altogether, reliving it becomes the task of a person whose proximity to events was immediate and perhaps shielded by the innocence of youth. Such is the story to follow, told by a son who uncovered the details decades after the death of the father. The records he left behind were sufficient to tell the story relatively accurately for the years when the author was a child. The later years are supplemented with first-hand participation in the life of the subject.

This is a very personal story of an engineer whose work took him from Germany, through France, and to the United States. Engineers do not often write of their work, but the reasons for putting this experience on paper are compelling because they have historical significance. These creative individuals usually let the products of their creativity speak for themselves. Products tell a good story, but generally without the human dimension woven into them. This engineer, as well as others like him, were at the center of aviation engine development in the middle of the twentieth century. Their work led to the present state of aviation and the mobility that aviation provides. The turbulence of war and the disruption imposed on the lives of those who were lucky enough to have survived it are central to this narrative.

This history starts in the midst of what some historians describe as the twentieth century's "Thirty Years' War," the years 1914 to 1945. The linking of World War I and World War II is hard to argue against. This period may be defined by two bullets shot from two guns. The first one was fired in Sarajevo in July 1914, and the other in a Berlin bunker in April 1945. The interbellum period after World War I set the stage for yet another war because the victors were inept at dealing with the peacemaking process. The "Great War" was not to be "The War to End All Wars."

War is made by specific individuals in government and is suffered by everyone else. Even as World War I is finished, the ordinary Germans who had nothing to do with the events are punished for war "reparations," as if such a process could actually be devised. Yes, structures can be rebuilt but lost lives cannot be undone. The Treaty of Versailles of 1919 had hard economic consequences on Germans in the 1920s. Thus the stage was set for much that was to follow.

The twentieth century is characterized by turbulence that had an impact on millions of people, many millions. The technological component of that history also left its mark on the world of today. Specifically, a thorough understanding of the technology involved in the production of power from fuel-burning engines constitutes a late chapter of the Industrial Revolution. It is hard to understate the importance of that dimension of technology. As applied to mobility, the breakthroughs that were made on land with the invention of the internal combustion engine and later with the jet engine in air are integral parts of modern life and warfare.

The jet engine is primarily the product of thinkers and tinkerers in Great Britain and Germany. The associated field as a technology arose and came to a sort of maturity during the Second World War. It is explored here in the form of a biography of one German individual who made his mark in it. The telling of that story requires a description of the world as it was when this individual and his colleagues entered it, so that their roles can be understood. To that end, we begin with the state of the art in the 1930s and necessarily talk about engines and their characteristics, albeit from a layman's perspective. While illustrations are used to describe engines, the reader may discover technical details and jargon in other sources.

CHAPTER 2

Beginnings and Hugo Junkers

A bit of relevant history had already been established by the mid-1930s. Because the name Junkers will play a prominent role, a few words about the man will set the stage. In the history of airplanes and airplane engines, Hugo Junkers (1859–1935) was a German aviation pioneer whose influence is important from technical and industrial viewpoints. He formed an aircraft building concern, and a number of important innovations are to his credit. His first venture was Junkers Motorenbau, with a focus on building aircraft engines in Magdeburg starting in 1913. That was followed in 1918 by another endeavor: Junkers Flugzeugwerk located in Dessau (about 45 miles southeast of Magdeburg).

His aviation interests predated World War I and persisted throughout his life. His work centered on the three dimensions of aviation: airplane construction, engines, and operation of air transport services. The latter had to be carried out within the severe limitations imposed on Germany by the Treaty of Versailles. The treaty forbade any activity that had potential military purposes. Junkers nevertheless saw a future in commercial aviation and fought the treaty limitations as best he could. The literature is replete with his efforts at building viable commercial and sport aircraft. Good airplanes needed good design ideas. His included an early use of all-metal airframe construction (1915). The use of corrugated sheet iron (yes, iron!) is associated with Junkers, as is the later and widely used corrugated aluminum that is so characteristic of the airplanes of that time. He pioneered low wing monoplane design ideas that were widely adopted by others. The motivation to increase airplane speed centered on the need to do away with the biplane wing design of the day and the associated struts and wires that produce so much drag.

As soon as hostilities ceased after World War I, he saw that peaceful opportunities in aviation were promising. To that end, his company built a robust and reliable airplane. The F 13 was a single-engine, all-metal airplane, sporting the well-known corrugated metal skin. It was small, able to carry four passengers with a crew of two. The cockpit was open with a windshield, while the passengers sat in an enclosed cabin. An important design novelty was the use of a single cantilever wing without struts.

The F 13 entered flight service in 1920. It functioned so well that the following year, Junkers established the airline Junkers Luft Verkehr to use about sixty of these airplanes. This airline merged with Deutsche Luft Hansa in 1926 to become Lufthansa, which is still in operation today.

The successful F 13 was built until 1932, both in Germany and licensed to other countries, partially because more powerful engines could be installed and such installations required them to be carried out outside Germany (because of treaty restrictions). About 322 F 13s were built and operated around the world.

The 1924–25 period saw the introduction of a more capable airplane, the G 23, and later the more powerful G 24 trimotor. These airplanes had an enclosed cockpit and were a follow-on development of the F 13. They carried a crew of two with fourteen passengers. Like the older model, the G23/24 was entangled in arguments about its utility for military purposes when it was built. Consequently, some twenty or so were built in Sweden, in addition to the seventy-two produced in Germany.

A not-so-successful large airplane project was the Junkers G 38. It first flew in November 1929. The airplane was of a blended wing and fuselage design, where the wing of the monoplane was sufficiently thick to allow the cabin passengers to sit in it with a forward and downward view of the passing landscape. Unusual features of the design were a biplane tail and dissimilar engines on each wing. In the early 1930s, the G 38 was the largest transport airplane flown. It had a large wingspan (~144 ft.) and a wing area about equal to that of the Boeing 707-320. Only two G 38s were built. The market had vanished in the worldwide depression after the stock market crash of 1929.

The difficult economic times of the 1920s in Germany led Junkers to sell off other assets to preserve his aviation company. The company struggled. In addition, the lack of a market for the large G 38 led Junkers to return to smaller, more modest aircraft. The Ju 52 was the focus of further work. It started as a single-engine airplane but was soon re-engined with three air-cooled engines. While Junkers Motorenbau continued to produce liquid-cooled engines, the switch to air cooling

The Junkers G 38, an unsuccessful large passenger airliner. Note the fixed landing gear and the biplane horizontal tail. From a postcard sent by Sig to his future wife in 1936.

A Junkers Ju 52. *Courtesy Lufthansa Bildarchiv, Photo: Bodo Bondzio*

on the Ju 52 presaged increasing and wide use in commercial aviation. In Germany, civil aviation was effectively reborn with the introduction of the Ju 52 all-metal airliner in 1932. This airplane was a very successful design produced in large numbers. For a time ending around 2008, the modern, jet-powered Lufthansa maintained a vintage Ju 52 trimotor airplane (D-AQUI) for nostalgic flights and still retains it for its historical value.

CHAPTER 3

The Limited Piston Engines and Their Propellers

By first looking at the history of airplanes and their engines, we can anticipate the intersection between the Junkers company and the lives of Sig and his colleagues. This intersection necessarily involves a description of some technical dimensions of airplane propulsion and of the military situation in Germany before World War II. Sig joined Junkers after the death of Hugo Junkers, so that Junkers will just be the name of a company that the Nazi government took over and turned into a producer of military hardware bearing the Junkers name: airplanes and engines. Earlier attempts at government interference in the production affairs of Junkers were actively and successfully resisted because he was very much opposed to the Nazis and was a pacifist by nature.

The performance boundaries of the ordinary piston engines first used for powering airplanes, be they water- or air-cooled, were well understood. The persistent goal of engine builders was to obtain more power with a lighter-weight machine. At a fundamental level, the ability of a piston-cylinder engine to provide power is limited by the amount of air it can process. To be specific, the ability to flow air into and out of the cylinder volume is strongly constrained by the small flow areas provided by the valves as they open. The air speed past these valves cannot exceed sonic speeds. Thus engines are operated at as large a displacement as practical and at as high a rotational speed as allowed by the flow past valves.

This is the site of the fundamental limitation of getting air from the intake manifold into the cylinder volume past the larger intake valve. From a sectioned Pratt & Whitney R-4360 engine at the Smithsonian National Air and Space Museum.

In addition to the engine performance limitations, the airplane suffered a limitation of its own when it uses a propeller to provide thrust. The propeller tip could not be allowed to approach the speed of sound, lest it suffer very large drag increases and the associated demand for more power. Thus, yet another limitation on flight speed is imposed by the air's compressibility and its finite speed of sound.

These limitations spawned considerable work on designs that allow for higher engine and airplane performance. For the airplane, performance is largely measured by attainable speed. Much of the work in the field of aviation during and after World War II was centered on meeting the challenge of flying faster. During the piston engine era, the flight speeds of military aircraft in service could not approach the 600- to-700-mile-per-hour speed of sound in air.

The first step in solving the power problem was to push piston engines for more power. Without going into the many avenues that were pursued, it is easy to imagine that every opportunity was examined and that some of these were very effective. Supercharging and turbocharging were developed. These allowed airplanes to fly not just faster but higher. Valving was improved with arrangements that involved more than a single intake and single exhaust valve. Sleeve valves were tried and used. Novel piston, cylinder, and crankshaft arrangements were tried, all with the goal of increasing power. Among these were multi-row radial engines, W-engines, X-engines, horizontally opposed H-engines to supplement the more conventional radial, V-, and in-line or I-engines. Finally, the power of the hot exhaust was put to good use by incorporating it into mechanisms that added jet thrust rather than just being exploited by a turbocharger or simply wasted.

None of these efforts were successful in overcoming the flight speed limit of the propeller-driven airplane.

CHAPTER 4

The Jet Engine

Ideas and experiments that will find a place in the history of the jet engine had been around for a few decades. The coalescence of such ideas ultimately resulted in the development of the jet engine in Germany and the eventual realization of the first operational military jet airplane. The concepts related to the jet engine were also explored elsewhere, notably in Great Britain, but the focus here is on the effort in Germany and specifically those related to the Junkers jet engine, the Jumo 004.

All work on jet engines in Germany ended in 1945 but was carried on around the world—in part by the German engineers in this story. For a comprehensive history of jet engine development, including technical details, the reader will be well rewarded by looking at the referenced books by Antony L. Kay. Kay examines in great detail the work done during and after the war by the various countries, companies, and individuals who can claim a place in that history.

The 1930s were a time when individuals in German academic and industrial institutions made significant progress in the understanding of the physics of fluid motion. Any textbook on aerodynamics will reveal the names of a number of Germans associated with specific physical understanding. The names Prandtl, Busemann, Schlichting, Kutta, and (much earlier) Mach come to mind. It is this environment that allowed people to think in terms of a jet propulsion system for airplanes.

The notion of producing jet thrust, rather than power for a propeller, was intriguing. From a technical perspective, we might note that the propeller-imposed speed limit might be overcome in an airplane that produced only a jet as propulsive thrust—no propeller. This idea was realized by the Italian airplane builder Caproni with his model Campini N.1, built and flown in 1940. The airplane used a modest power V-12 piston engine to drive a variable pitch fan inside the tube-shaped fuselage. An afterburner was provided to add to the thrust produced. For a time, Caproni could claim to have flown the first "jet" airplane. He was to learn later that a real jet airplane with a gas turbine engine had been flown (secretly) the previous year in Germany. The Caproni airplane was underpowered and did not find a place in service.

About the time that Caproni was building his N.1 airplane, the engineers at Junkers were thinking along similar lines: drive a compressor with a conventional, perhaps modified, internal combustion engine. A number of options were considered, including free piston engines, among others. The idea was to use a compressor of the type developed at the AVA in Göttingen. The AVA (Aerodynamische Versuchsanstalt) was an aeronautical research institution created in 1907 by the famous aerodynamicist Ludwig Prandtl, who ran it until 1937. At the AVA, the basic research necessary for a practical axial flow compressor came to light. Such a compressor was considered a necessary element for the new type of jet engine in the late 1930s.

It occurred to a number of investigators, among them Hans von Ohain, Frank Whittle, and others, that one might have to abandon the idea of using the internal combustion engine altogether. Among the others were the people at Junkers. There, the goal of a "special construction bureau" was to develop an engine where a significant part of the performance was jet thrust, in addition to power for a propeller. The initial attempts at a new engine type were toward a turboprop, using the gas turbine as the prime mover.

In 1934, the director of the new engine effort at Junkers was Dr. Herbert Wagner, working in Dessau. He also supervised a team of engineers at the Junkers engine plant in Magdeburg. These two entities were combined in 1936, after founder Hugo Junkers's death, into Junkers Flugzeug- und Mototenwerke (JFM)—a single company with two divisions.

Wagner recognized the limitations of the propeller on an airplane and redirected the development effort to an engine that produces only jet thrust. What was needed was a steady flow engine that burned fuel in a constant pressure process, like that in an oil burner. The ideas and the technology were around but not yet with sufficiently useful performance to be practical. An early technology example might have provided motivation. In 1937, the Swiss Brown-Boveri Company was selling so-called Velox oil burners for steam powerplants. The Velox burner functionally resembled what we call a gas turbine engine today: a compressor, a compact burner, and a gas turbine. This burner supplies hot combustion gas to a steam generator. While the function of this burner is to deliver hot air to a boiler rather than jet thrust, it was similar in principle. All that was necessary was to improve the performance of the compressor and turbine to enable it to work with higher gas temperatures and with higher aerodynamic efficiencies. Throughout the history of the development of the gas turbine, the reality was that high temperature at the turbine inlet was desirable and necessary for good performance. Achieving that was a difficult challenge for the design of the turbine. Today, these challenges are successfully met and developed further with sophisticated metallurgy in the blades and fancy cooling techniques.

Wagner tried to obtain financial support for this work from the German Air Ministry (Reichsluftfahrtministerium—yes, four words rolled into one, abbreviated RLM) and was turned down, so Junkers continued funding the effort. In 1938, he was granted a patent for the basic turbojet (German patent no. 724,091: "Thrust Installation for Aircraft") that grew out of the turboprop development. This patent was undoubtedly kept as a state secret. A running engine was developed using gaseous propane as a fuel to avoid the vaporization issues associated with the use of a more conventional liquid fuel. That challenge would be solved later. Sadly, the engine's performance was so disappointing that the effort in Magdeburg was discontinued in 1939.

Dr. Anselm Franz, working in Dessau, was tasked with the development of novel reciprocating engine concepts. Dessau was the locale of the aircraft part of the company. Engine work was centered in Magdeburg. Franz was also competent to evaluate the work on the jet engine. His assessment, made in August 1939, was harsh and realistic and motivated the Dessau engineers to continue work on improving the Magdeburg engine. At this point in time, Franz concluded that for the power required, the internal combustion engine in any form was too heavy and the gas turbine engine was a better bet. He and others had no illusions about the difficulties facing them. The development of a high-temperature turbine was going to be challenging if the engine was to perform well in terms of power output and fuel consumption. The fuel usage issue was recognized as critical if the jet was going to surpass the piston engine for aircraft propulsion.

It was during this time that the RLM became interested in the jet engine and agreed to fund further development at Junkers. The director of the Dessau works, Otto Mader, in spite of the challenges brought out by Franz, agreed to continue jet engine work, but at only one facility: Dessau. The resultant management turmoil led the principals of the Magdeburg effort to resign and go elsewhere. Wagner left to pursue other interests, and most of the engineers went to Heinkel, where RLM-funded work was available on a competitive engine. The task of jet engine work in Dessau fell to Franz, who had to build a new team of engineers for this purpose. The people he gathered would be the principals of this story, including Siegfried Decher and Wolfgang Stein. Dr. Heinrich Adenstedt would also join that team as the only significant person from the Magdeburg group.

The RLM funding of the Junkers program led to a thorough review of prior work to address problem areas. The resulting ideas ultimately found their way into the Jumo 004 engine. The central idea of an uncomplicated jet engine like the 004 is that if a jet is to be produced, the engine's function is in the role of a pump to increase the pressure of the air it handles. As in any pump-like device, a means had to be devised to raise the air pressure. The engine community was split on whether the best way involved the use of the *radial flow* compressor, as von Ohain did in his engine, or look to the *axial flow* compressor (available from the AVA work) that was more challenging but much more promising. The engineers at Junkers facing their task had no illusions that this was going to be easy and yield an engine that would be light enough for airplane application.

The Jumo 004 did not, however, arise in isolation, because a concerted effort was made by the German Air Ministry to identify the best way to build such an engine. The lines to follow describing the RLM effort lean heavily on the existing literature. The volume by von Gersdorff and the books by Kay listed in the bibliography were the source of much of the material presented here.

CHAPTER

5

Von Ohain and the First Jet Flight

The history of the jet engine cannot be told without getting into a few technical aspects of engine design. These include performance parameters such as thrust, pressure ratio, bypass ratio, among others. These technical descriptors will be invoked only in general terms and hopefully lucidly. The various iterations on component arrangements examined in the years before and during World War II will necessarily be part of the discussion. The best way to configure a gas turbine engine was not evident at the beginning of the period that can be described as the jet engine's childhood.

First, a little background. Propulsion of an aircraft requires the use of a system consisting of an engine and aerodynamic components to take in the air and to exhaust it as a jet. The engine must deliver exhaust gas at an elevated pressure to enable the production of the jet. The aerodynamic components are an inlet that supplies air to the engine and a nozzle to accelerate the high-pressure exhaust gas. Newton's laws state that the increase of the speed (momentum actually) of the jet relative to the incoming air will produce the thrust force necessary to overcome airplane drag.

The challenge was to build a practical system with a new type of engine. One aspect has to do with the thermodynamics (heat management) of the engine and another with the performance of the necessary components, the compressor in particular.

The thermodynamics requires three things to be performed reasonably well in order for the engine to function. Its compressor has to be efficient, and in addition, the turbine must also be efficient to drive the compressor. By "efficiency," we mean that a minimum of the work involved in either driving the compressor or that produced by the turbine ends up as wasted heat. The engine also has to burn fuel in a reasonably compact, steady, and reliable way, with the combustion gas temperature acceptable to the turbine for its survival. These were the challenges facing the individuals dreaming about an entirely new engine type.

In looking at German jet engine literature in the wartime period, one is often confronted with the abbreviated letters "TL." The letters are from a German acronym description of what we call a jet engine today. The letters stand for "*T*urbinen—*L*uftstrahlantrieb." A "Luftstrahl" is an air jet, and "Antrieb" is German for "propulsion." Hence the purpose of TL is to denote jet propulsion by means of a gas turbine engine, in contrast to the Caproni idea of using an internal combustion engine. In addition to this label, the German engineers used ZTL and PTL for bypass and turboprop engines. The "Z" refers to two (zwei) streams, while the "P" refers to a propeller.

In 1936–37, Hans von Ohain, who had worked with Ludwig Prandtl at the University of Göttingen, had interested airplane builder Ernst Heinkel in an idea that he developed. Von Ohain's interest lay in the interaction of energy and fluid flow and showed the promise of jet propulsion. The contact between Heinkel and von Ohain was established by Professor Robert Pohl. Heinkel was interested and hired von Ohain to design an engine based on these new ideas. Heinkel also took on Max Hahn, who was von Ohain's very able mechanical assistant. As a matter of interest, it should be noted that von Ohain's academic work completed in 1933 consisted of a design for an optical microphone, whereby sound could be recorded on movie film. The patent he obtained for that work was sold to the Siemens Company. Von Ohain redirected the monies he received to his interest in jet engines. He was an inventive young man!

When describing the performance of engines, the central aspect is the propulsive force produced: the engine thrust. The easiest way to state the thrust of an engine is at sea-level conditions (rather than at altitude and at speed) in a stationary test stand where measurements are easily made. In this writing, measures of thrust will be depicted in the US standard of pounds of force. Other units are used by adherents to the metric system.

The first functional von Ohain test engine was the He S 2. Here the letters in the name were chosen to describe the Heinkel Strahltriebwerk (Heinkel jet propulsion engine). It was fired with hydrogen to make combustion reliable and produced 286 pounds of thrust. An improved model He S 3, burning vaporized liquid fuel and producing 1,100 pounds, followed in March 1938. Heinkel was very anxious to let the engine fly and built the He 178 airplane. The airplane was not intended for a military purpose; rather, it was merely to demonstrate the potential of the jet engine. The jet age dawned on August 27, 1939, with a six-minute flight near Rostock. The airplane would later be lost to history in the bombing of Germany during World War II.

Thus it was that von Ohain, a young man in his late twenties, became the central force behind the construction of the jet engine for the Heinkel He 178. The interest in such an engine for flight propulsion was nascent more or less simultaneously in England and Germany. The English story centered on Frank Whittle is a very interesting tale of its own.

A look at the general engine configurations allows for interesting conclusions regarding their application in an aircraft. The relatively large diameter is a consequence of the radial flow compressor and the radial flow turbine in the He S 3 engine. A single axial-flow stage initiates the compression process, which is completed with the radial flow impeller and a diffuser. The diffuser is an air duct of increasing flow area, so that the flow slows down and a pressure rise is realized (as demanded by the Bernoulli principle). This engine was unique for its use of a radial (in) flow turbine. The axial flow turbine was later preferred in all other engines built in Germany and in Great Britain at that time. Today, the axial turbine design is nearly universal.

In order to be clear about the nature of a radial flow compressor, the image below (top left) shows the salient part—namely the rotor. It takes in air from the left and, by means of the vanes shown, hurls it out radially in all directions. The air is then collected in a diffuser. To illustrate further how such an impeller is used, the example shown (on the top right) is a World War II vintage (1943) General Electric I-40 engine employing a double-sided rotor.

The lower figures show the contrast in compressor design with a single rotor disk of an axial flow compressor. The air flow is in the general direction of the shaft rotation axis, although in reality, the flow path is

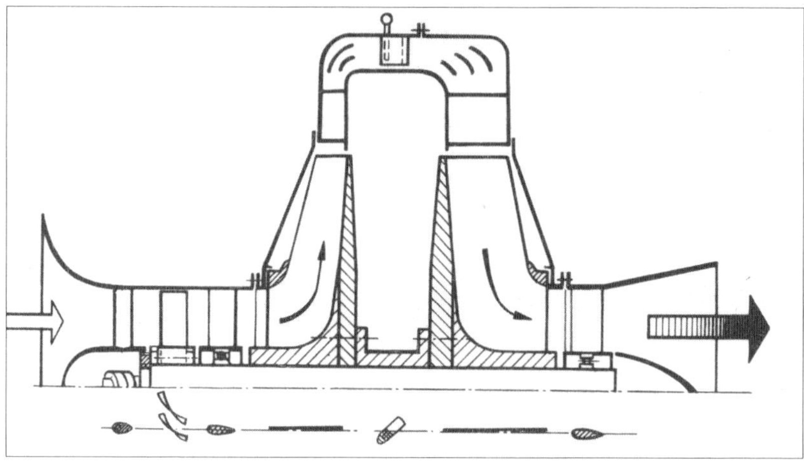

The von Ohain-Heinkel He S 2 preflight test engine. In all sketches to follow, the air flow through the engine is from left to right. *Kyrill von Gersdorff / Kurt Grasmann, Flugmotoren und Strahltriebwerke, Ausgabe 1981, Bernard & Graefe Verlag, Koblenz, Bonn, Bad Neuenahr-Ahrweiler*

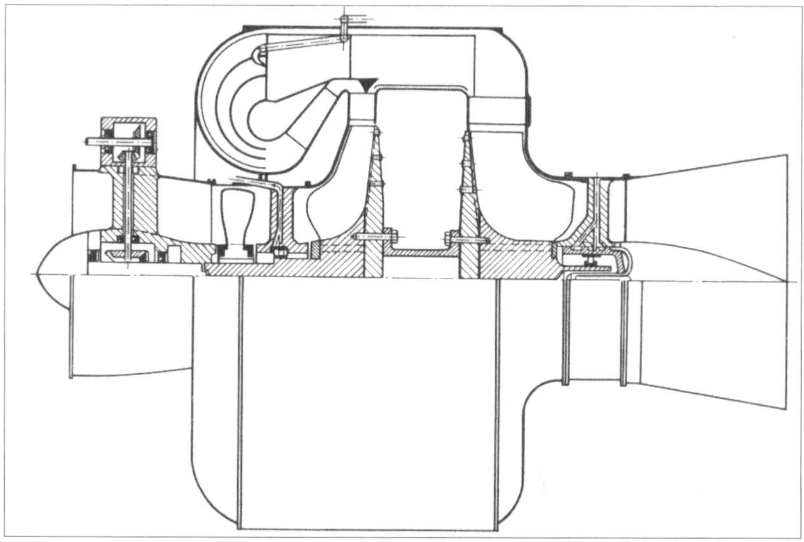

The von Ohain-Heinkel He S 3 engine that launched the jet age. *Kyrill von Gersdorff / Kurt Grasmann*

helical. In an axial flow compressor, a second set of blades, called *stators*, serve as a diffuser. In practice, diffusion takes place in both rotor and stator blading. An engine application showing an axial flow compressor is shown on the bottom right. This particular engine, cut open for the purpose of viewing its components, is a Lycoming T53—an engine that

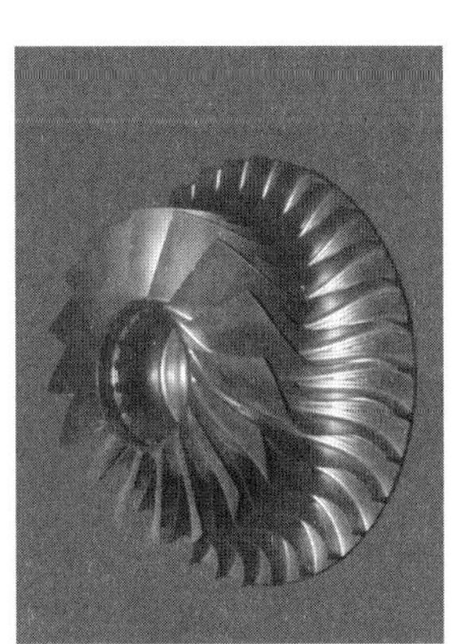

Rotor for a radial flow compressor (*top left*) and a GE I-40 engine (*top right*), wherein a double-sided radial rotor is used. (*Courtesy of General Electric*) On the bottom left is a single rotor of an axial flow compressor. Note the blades are oriented to allow the flow in the compressor case to be helical in direction. A Lycoming T53 engine compressor (*bottom right*) showing a combination of multistage axial and a single radial stage. Note that the axial portion has (difficult to see) stationary (stators, affixed to the case) vanes between rotors. *Kyrill von Gersdorff / Kurt Grasmann*

will arise later in our story. It is somewhat unusual in that the compressor is partly an axial flow compressor followed by a radial one.

Both compressors and turbines are called *dynamic flow machines* because they involve flow velocity changes with corresponding pressure changes. The turbine may be thought of as the reverse of a compressor. In the turbine, flow is accelerated to high speed to impact a rotor that uses aerodynamic forces to obtain mechanical power. The flow acceleration, the conversion of thermal energy to speed by the decreasing pressure, takes place first in a stationary set of blades, called a *turbine nozzle,* whose function is the opposite of a diffuser. The aerodynamic design and function of a turbine are significantly easier than that of a compressor—hence the emphasis on the development work necessary for the travails of the compressor. Air simply does not like to flow into a region of high pressure. Great care has to be employed to force it to do so. On the other hand, in the turbine, air loves to flow to a region of lower pressure.

CHAPTER 6

The RLM Contracts

In order to do justice to the events as they relate to German jet engine developments, we have to delve a bit into the history of the Luftwaffe's involvement, as well as the dilemmas engineers faced regarding how best to build the jet engine. To that end, we summarize both of these facets of the story to set the stage for the story to come. The major technical issue at hand involved a choice between two kinds of air compressors that might be suitable. Both had advantages and disadvantages, and neither had yet been used in an engine that was potentially good enough for military purposes.

In German industrial and academic circles, a number of conferences were held in the years following 1936, concluding that engines for jet thrust production were not only desirable but possible. There had been progress in a number of countries regarding the understanding of how an axial compressor might work. Such work was carried out during the 1920s and 1930s, primarily for the field of electric power generation. This technical progress was followed by the RLM by two individuals who were central to the promotion of engines for high-speed military aircraft within the RLM. In 1938 (while von Ohain at Heinkel was secretly running successful engine tests), Helmut Schelp and Hans Mauch toured the various laboratories and found a degree of skepticism that the challenges facing such a new engine type could be overcome. In part, the concern was that reciprocating engine development work at the various engine firms was keeping them very occupied. Further, there were concerns that the efficiencies of the compressor and turbine might be insufficient for a practical engine. Nevertheless, BMW and Brandenburg

Motoren Werke (Bramo) were intrigued. This led Schelp and the RLM to originate a development program (1939) to investigate a number of aspects of these new engines. In that same year, BMW acquired Bramo, and with that purchase, the technical staff at BMW grew with, among others, Hermann Oestrich, who was with Bramo at the time. With growing RLM interest, other manufacturers became intrigued by the technical possibilities and for business reasons.

Yet there was a major wrinkle: What was the best way to compress the air? Here we have to address technical details, albeit lightly. Whittle and von Ohain had used a *radial* type of compressor that worked but was fundamentally limiting. It could only raise the pressure by modest amounts, and more pressure would be needed if really powerful engines were to be built. The design of the compressor for these first engines was awkward. It was only moderately efficient, bulky, and thus not easily amenable to building a sleek airplane.

The axial flow compressor was an alternative. The Junkers and BMW engineers pursued building their relatively simple engine configurations with this better compressor type. Jumping ahead to the present, we note that the fat, relatively easy-to-run, but pressure-deficient radial flow compressor is all but relegated to history. The axial flow compressor is now in near-universal use in jet engines for aircraft of all types.

The axial flow compressor engine was challenging to build and operate. The operational difficulty is connected with the need for a control system that keeps the airflow orientation relative to the angle of the blades within a narrow range so that the flow does not stall and so that operation is efficient. There was sufficient technical optimism that an engine based on its use was practical. The firms Junkers and BMW proposed to build engines with this type of compressor.

The RLM funded a development program that was a broad attack on understanding the technology of the gas turbine as a propulsion system. It included a number of projects numbered TL-109-00n, with a number of important aspects to be investigated, all aimed at devising a practical aircraft jet engine and bringing to light the relative merits of the two compressor types. Here, the projects will be labeled as "-00n," omitting the TL 109 portion of the designation. An advanced He S 3 to be called the He S 8 at Heinkel was project -001. This engine was to have a radial flow compressor and turbine, building on the initial success of the He S 3. Heinkel's interest in the subject was no longer a secret!

In project -002, BMW was to examine an axial flow compressor with counterrotating blading. The investigation into counter-rotating blading proposed in -002 was motivated by the thought that having both kinds of blading put power into the flow would make for a lighter, more compact compressor. The mechanical arrangement is, however, very complicated and never saw the light of day.

The reality that the axial compressor utilizes two kinds of blading requires a brief discussion of how it functions. In the axial compressors we commonly use today, the flow encounters alternating rows of blading, where one set rotates and the following set is stationary within the engine. Such a blading row combination is called a stage. The rotor blading is designed to accelerate the flow in the direction of rotation while decreasing the flow speed within the blade row. This increases pressure, as demanded by the Bernoulli principle. This sounds incredible, but a look at engineering velocity diagrams for such a machine should help clear the matter. Such a look is reserved for the technically hardy reader. The stator blade row redirects the flow in the direction opposite of rotation and also slows the flow down, increasing the pressure further. With these events, the flow leaves the stator more or less in the direction it entered the rotor (but at higher pressure), and the process can be repeated as often as necessary.

The pressure rises in the two elements of a stage are modest, on the order of 5–15 percent, because the process is delicate—again because air does not like to flow into a region of higher pressure. This dimension of the compressor has two consequences. The first is that higher pressure ratios, desired for thermodynamic reasons, will require many stages in a compressor. The second consequence is that great care has to be exercised so that changes in operating conditions do not lead to any stalling. All of the axial flow compressor projects funded by the RLM have a considerable number of stages, with or without counterrotating stators.

Project -003 was also a BMW undertaking under Hermann Oestrich for a fairly simple jet engine to be known as the BMW 003. By "simple" we mean that the engine consists of only four components: axial compressor, burner turbine, and nozzle. An inlet is also provided.

Project -004 was for a similar design headed by Anselm Franz at Junkers. This effort ultimately resulted in the only German production jet engine to be called the Jumo 004.

A Porsche -005 was also considered as a means for propelling a short-life cruise missile.

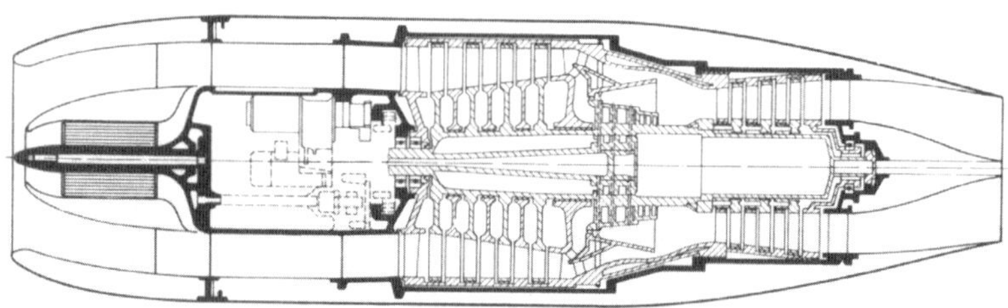

The BMW-002 counter-rotating compressor jet engine. The heavy black lined structure is a rotating external case consisting of a turbine and the compressor that is driven by it. *Kyrill von Gersdorff / Kurt Grasmann*

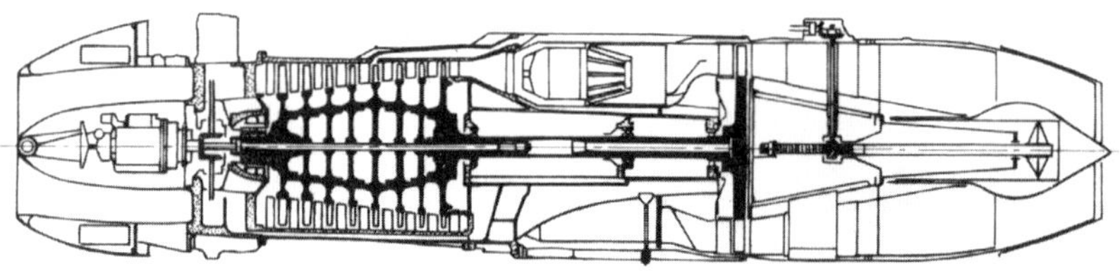

Cross section of the Jumo 004. Note the simplicity of the design and its streamlined shape. Airflow is from left to right. Eight compressor stages are used, driven by a single turbine. *Kyrill von Gersdorff / Kurt Grasmann*

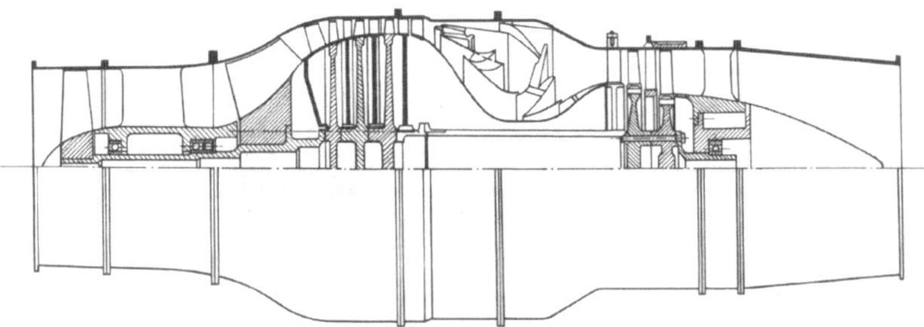

The Heinkel He S 11 engine with partial use of a diagonal flow compressor. This design was funded by Heinkel and not part of TL-109. *Kyrill von Gersdorff / Kurt Grasmann*

Project -006 was a Heinkel undertaking for a new engine to be called the He S 30, in which the compressor was of an axial flow design, departing from the radial design of earlier Heinkel engines.

[8] The development of the He S 30 was preceded by a number of designs, including that of the He S 11, which featured an unusual approach in the compressor. It was a combination of one axial stage, a "diagonal" stage, and three further axial stages. The diagonal compressor resembles a radial flow impeller, with the difference being that the flow leaves at an angle roughly halfway between the radial and the axial directions. The advantage gained was a pressure ratio of 4.4, well better than values around 3.0 achieved by radial designs. The design was also slimmer than a pure radial flow compressor engine. The He S 11 was to be a more powerful engine, with a thrust of about 2,900 pounds, but failed to interest the RLM.

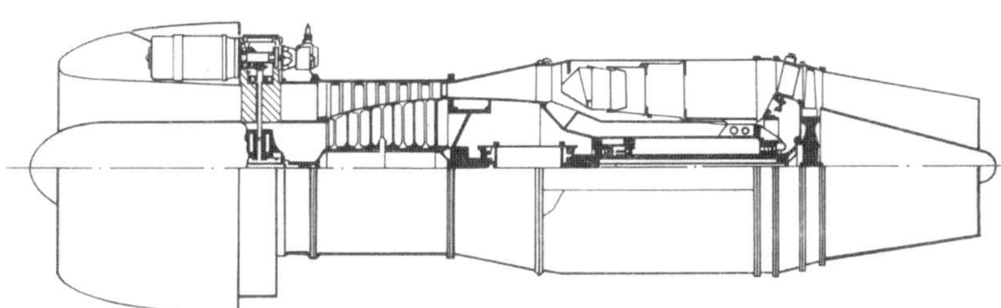

Cross-section of the TL-109-006 engine, also known as a He S 30. Note the absence of a flow control on the nozzle. This engine is quite similar to the Junkers and BMW project proposals. *Kyrill von Gersdorff / Kurt Grasmann*

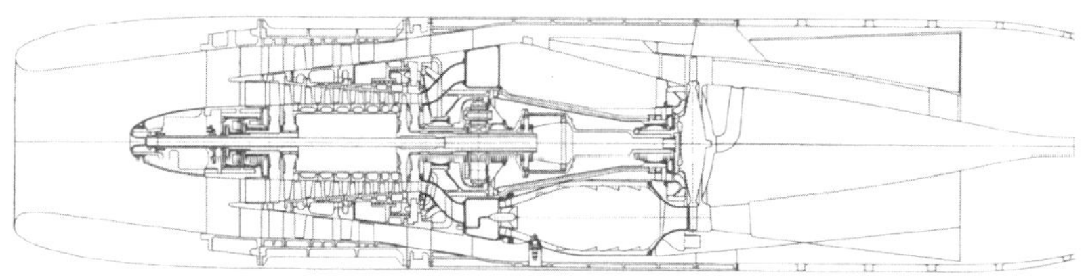

A bypass engine configuration investigated by Daimler Benz as project DB-007. A mixer ahead of the exit nozzle combines the bypass and hot flows. *Kyrill von Gersdorff / Kurt Grasmann*

The last of the initial group of projects was a Daimler Benz study and the construction of a two-stream (bypass) engine, including a counter-rotating compressor, a bypass ratio of 0.7, and an ambitious compressor pressure ratio of 8 from a 17-stage compressor. The -007 project was designed to explore greater thrust with reduced fuel consumption using the bypass concept. Unlike the ca. 1,750 pounds of thrust from some of the other turbojet projects in process, the anticipated goal was to realize about 3,000 pounds.

In addition to these projects, there were ultimately a significant number of other engine projects involving the companies that carried out work in the early phases. Most of these were immature design exercises with uncertain production prospects.

CHAPTER 7

Priority Realignment

In mid-1940, the general staff of the Wehrmacht came to believe that the war would not last long and that every effort had to be made to win quickly. That included focusing on the production of hardware that was currently useful and in production. All projects with a long-term realization were to be suspended until after the war. It did not take long for the staff to realize that the war was not going all that well. Luftwaffe General Adolf Galland argued for the practicality and superiority of jet fighters over conventional aircraft. That view was ultimately accepted for a reinvigorated development of jet engines. A decision was made in early 1941 by Schelp and the RLM to pursue jets by focusing an emphasis on projects -003 and -004, to the detriment of the others. These two engines were foreseen as powerplants for the Me 262 (twin-jet fighter) and the Ar 234 (bomber). They also powered a number of other, less significant, aircraft. The team also recognized the need to pursue compressor designs for higher-pressure ratios in order to allow the designs of bypass and turboprop engines. In that environment, the radial flow compressor (-001) and counter-rotating axial flow (-002) projects were canceled in late 1942. The bypass engine support was substantially reduced, although it appears to have been pursued by Daimler at a low level. The Porsche (-005) project was canceled. The He S 30 engine (-006) was not pursued in favor of the BMW 003 and Jumo 004 that were similar in layout. Heinkel, as an airplane builder, had hoped to use his engines in an He 280, a twin jet fighter similar to the Me 262. A small number of these were built, and the airplane project was finally canceled in early 1943.

The prioritization of this time also led to preliminary funding of more ambitious follow-on projects to the BMW 003 and the Jumo 004, for even better performance. The first-generation engines had projected thrust levels of around 2,000 pounds. Preliminary design work on Jumo 012 and BMW 018 turbojets and a number of turboprops was authorized. In general, the -012 and -018 engines were to be larger and more powerful than the -004 and -003 engines. Pressure ratios that were used in the first-engine generation were on the order of 3.1, now raised to around six with an increase in the number of compressor stages from 7 and 8 to 11 and 12. Thrust levels were to be boosted to more than 6,500 pounds. These engines would allow for the design of airplanes with significantly improved performance. These ambitious plans were ultimately terminated with the end of war hostilities, although the Junkers TL 109-012 was built in Russia by the Junkers engineers who were unfortunate enough to have stayed in the Soviet Occupation Zone. A turboprop version of the -012 engine (PTL 109-022) was looking toward an engine with propeller power levels near 9,000 horsepower! Such a power level was multiples of the power levels available from piston/cylinder engines of the day. Looking ahead to the postwar years, we note that the 28-cylinder Pratt & Whitney R-4360 took the still-standing power prize for that engine technology, with a capability of about 4,000 horsepower. These words illustrate that performance for jet and piston engines is measured in fundamentally different ways. Jet engines produce thrust (in pounds), whereas piston and turboprop engines are rated in terms of the horsepower they put out. Thus, a gas turbine engine can be compared to a jet engine only when there is a propeller involved. Otherwise, the two engine types live in their own domains.

The end of the war terminated all German development efforts in their tracks.

So it was that the Jumo 004 was developed and put into service in the simplest form that reality allowed and became a milestone in the history of technology. The key to its functional success was the use of a control system that allowed the compressor to function without pilot input. Improvements to future engines of greater complexity, such as the use of the bypass concept to improve fuel consumption, would come later. This approach paralleled that of Frank Whittle, who early on patented the idea of a bypass engine and let the idea lapse until such time that his pure turbojet was a reality.

The flow control system used by the Jumo 004 was developed by my father, Sig, the engineer near the center of this story. In any industrial setting, sole credit for an idea is not generally assignable to a single individual, but the issue of a patent makes it clear that most of the work may be credited to a specific person. In this case, the relevant patents (in Germany during the war and in the larger world later) for the control system are associated with Siegfried Decher and Wolfgang Stein. The latter's role was probably secondary, as patents usually require the names of two authors. Stein's contribution to the field of engine technology by the Junkers Yankees will be clearer as history unfolds.

The flow nozzle control mechanism embodied in the Jumo 004 was not to live long as new control methodologies were developed. However, the idea was carried over to France by the German engineers, and it was also accepted as a US patent, as our story will reveal. The French ATAR 101 engine was an advanced version of the BMW 003 developed under Hermann Oestrich. It used this form of control system up to the 101 C model. By 1948, the Jumo nozzle flow control technology was largely relegated to history. In its place, we see the use of compressor bleed valves, variable stator geometry, and sophisticated digital engine control systems used in modern engines.

The jet engine was a different kind of prime mover when compared to the internal combustion or piston engine. Jet engine performance levels are stated in terms of thrust force produced rather than horsepower. The Jumo 004 engine performance data illustrates that difference in that the power required of the turbine for the compressor was about 4,000 horsepower, while the engine produced about 2,000 pounds of thrust. These very large internal power levels cannot be compared to the power *output* from a piston engine, but they highlight the need to handle the transfer of power between turbine and compressor with high efficiency, because even small loss percentages involve large amounts of power.

As this is a story of the intersection of individuals and an important technology development, it is necessary to step back and look at the life course of my father, whose biography this writing is partially meant to be. While it would have been very satisfying to expand this writing by including more about the other individuals involved, that option was not available because the records have been out of reach. They may not even exist. The individuals themselves have all passed away in the seven decades after the war.

Introduction of the Man

Siegfried Heinrich August Decher was born in November 1912, joining an older sister, Annemarie, in the family. I shall refer to him as "Sig," the name he adopted in his professional life in the United States. To my mother, brother, and me, he was Papa. His world began in Darmstadt in Hesse Germany. He was probably "Siegfried" when his mother called him to come to the dinner table. His close German friends called him "Sigi."

Times were hard after World War I for Sig and his family. In short order, he, his older sister, and his mother became wards of the state in 1923, when Sig was only eleven, following the death of his father, Karl August Rudolf Decher. (Yes, it was customary in those days to have that many names.) Sig's father was an official in the city government of Darmstadt, and thus the family led an adequately comfortable life prior to the end of the war.

Siegfried H. Decher in the 1960s, from a passport picture

The reparation monies stipulated by the Versailles Treaty ending World War I robbed Germany of much of its economic strength and was designed to keep Germany from becoming powerful again. The early 1920s were, for Germany, a time of dysfunctional, albeit democratic, government and monetary inflation the likes of which were not to be experienced or appreciated by the victorious Western Allies. This aspect of the war's ending was better understood after World War II, the second phase of the modern Thirty Years'

A banknote issued in July 1923 redeemable in September. Such large denomination instruments served as currency during this time of severe inflation. The backside of this note is blank, as double-sided printing was unwarranted in this time when the value of the Reichsmark decreased so rapidly.

War. Inflation in the early 1920s was so severe that prices rose hourly and money had to be handled in voluminous bundles to pay for a loaf of bread. Then came the collapse of financial markets around the world, initiated by the American stock market crash in 1929.

For Germany, the situation was unbearable, and the political system spawned views of a better future from voices that spanned the political spectrum. The relation between economic and political well-being was not well appreciated at the time. Or perhaps it was, and the structural underpinnings of government were insufficient to be brought to bear on the needs of the time. On the economic side was the need for employment. Good economic circumstances demanded political stability. Political rigidity in the form of a single political party in power is indeed what Germany got, and with it came the second phase of the war that so dominated the history of the twentieth century. The relation between the economic and political spheres was better understood after World War II, when the Marshall Plan was devised in 1948.

It is not hard to imagine the connection between such a harsh environment and the health of a father charged with keeping a family going. Sig's father, Karl, died at age forty-six. Sig surmised that the very difficult work of coordinating administrative duties with a plethora of political parties and views in the difficult time after World War I led to his early death. His mother's strong religious conviction got her through the difficult years that followed. Because of the official role that Karl played while working in civil administration, the City of Darmstadt took care of his widow and her children with modest funds. This moderate support allowed them to remain in the home they occupied. The circumstances were, however, far from easy, but fortunately, they were not homeless.

As a youngster, Sig was a good student. He was well equipped to become an engineer because he was meticulous and disciplined in keeping records. That fact allowed this story to be told and also assured success in his professional engineering career. His transcripts from the Hessische Realgymnasium, which he attended from 1922 to 1931, were printed and with handwritten notes in the old Sütterlin writing style, now practically extinct. They summarized the progress of a good student. Official documents in that time and place were very formal, with many stamps, signatures, and even his picture displayed in the document. The modern German reader would likely be challenged by the now-obsolete handwriting style. The final transcript included a short summary of evaluations of all subjects covered. The American reader of today would also be surprised to see the topics covered in this evaluation: the first notation is a description of social behavior and the second refers to the degree of attention paid in class. Both were very good. The next important note concerns religion and, presumably, how well it was absorbed.

The subjects of mathematics, physics, chemistry, civics, geography, and biology were listed with their assessments—"good" or "very good." Several functional performance aspects of Sig's education in the gymnasium were also noted. These were drawing, music, and gymnastics, in the sense that a modern reader would understand that last word. The languages studied included German, as well as English and French as foreign languages. These were judged "On the whole, good." This system of evaluating students contrasts sharply with that employed by the author, who, a generation or two later, served on the faculty at the University of Washington, where the grading system was strictly numerical, employing about thirty grading steps. Such a fine gradation implies that a professor can actually determine the quality of a student's work to within a few percentage points of some imaginary ideal performance!

The religious training dimensions of Sig's education are still practiced in schools today, and in Sig's time, they were meant to direct the German student to a life cognizant of spiritual tradition and history. This was

Hessisches Realgymnasium zu Darmstadt

Zeugnis der Reife

für

Siegfried Heinrich August Lehr

geboren am 2. November 1912 zu Darmstadt

Sohn des Herrn Stadtamtmanns August Lehr †

zu Darmstadt, besuchte das Realgymnasium zu Darmstadt

von Ostern 1922 bis Ostern 1931

in den Klassen Sexta bis Oberprima

Der Oberprima gehörte er ein Jahr an.

Über sein Verhalten und seinen in der Reifeprüfung, beziehungsweise während des Schulbesuchs festgestellten Bildungsstand sind ihm nachstehende Noten erteilt worden:

Betragen: sehr gut

Aufmerksamkeit: sehr gut

Kenntnisse und Fertigkeiten:

In der Religionslehre: gut

Im Deutschen: gut

Im Lateinischen: im ganzen gut

Im Französischen: im ganzen gut

Im Englischen: im ganzen gut

In der Mathematik: sehr gut

This document is titled "Certificate of Maturity." Note the German handwriting and print style of the day. Note also the bar over the "u" to distinguish it from an "n" or even an "e." The word ahead of "gut" is "sehr," very. "Im ganzen" noted with the performance in languages means "on the whole."

In der darstellenden Geometrie (nach dem Ergebnis während des Schulbesuchs): —

In der Physik: gut

In der Chemie: gut

In der Geschichte: sehr gut

In der Staatsbürgerkunde: gut

In der Geographie: sehr gut

In der Biologie: —

Im Zeichnen (nach dem Ergebnis während des Schulbesuchs): gut

In der Musik (nach dem Ergebnis während des Schulbesuchs): gut

Im Turnen (nach dem Ergebnis während des Schulbesuchs): gut

Auf Grund vorstehender Noten ist dem Geprüften von dem Prüfungsausschuß das Zeugnis der Reife für höhere Berufsstudien erteilt worden.

Siegfried Ruhe wurde auf einstimmigen Beschluß des Lehrerrats ein Prämium zuerkannt für „gleichmäßige Pflichterfüllung und einwandfreies Verhalten während seiner ganzen Schulzeit". –

Dieses wird hierdurch amtlich beurkundet.

Darmstadt, am 26ten Februar 1931.

50 REICHSPFENNIG 50
STEMPEL-MARKE
VOLKSSTAAT HESSEN
7. MRZ. 1931

Der Prüfungsausschuß:

Volksstaat Hessen
Realgymnasium Darmstadt

...., Regierungsvertreter.

gez. } Ritsert, Oberstudiendirektor.

Für die Richtigkeit der ~~Abschrift~~:

Direktion des Realgymnasiums: Ritsert

Darmstadt, am 26ten Februar 1931.

Verzeichnis der Noten für Betragen: Sehr gut, gut, im ganzen gut, nicht ohne Tadel, tadelhaft.
„ „ „ „ Aufmerksamkeit und Leistungen: Sehr gut, gut, im ganzen gut, genügend, ungenügend.

meant to prepare the student for an understanding of what is required for a morally just and ethical life. How well that succeeded in the Hitler years to come is certainly an open question. For individuals like Sig, the role of the church and its efficacy as an institution to foster good behavior was severely constrained, probably deemed irrelevant to his young life and finally put to rest by the wartime experiences to come. His mother was apparently not very influential in molding his views as she was deeply religious. Whether and under what circumstances he rejected faith is not clear. In later life when I, as an adult, came closer to knowing him, he talked about and recognized that many Germans did indeed turn such learning into noble action during the Hitler years. Unfortunately, it was often ineffective and deadly. His views regarding the church will come up again later, particularly in the part of the narrative that depicts his move to the United States.

By the time of Sig's graduation, the economic and political situation in Germany was still in turmoil. Sig's family situation was such that he had to consider an effective means of earning a living. The family was rather poor financially, and the outside world was not much better. Germany still had an emasculated but real military. The year 1930 was before the military buildup by the National Socialists, but Sig found a way to get an engineering education via what military there was. Thus, before graduation, he applied for a traineeship in the Reichsmarine (the German navy, not yet called the Kriegsmarine). He hoped to get an engineering education at the government's expense. That would have entailed a commitment to military service, following any investment the government made in the students involved. In later years, Sig expressed to me his then wish was to join the submariners in the military after graduation. In August 1930, he learned that his application for Ingenieuroffizier (engineering officer) training was denied. He failed his physical exam. It seems that his physique would not be up to the rigors required by the service. Had he succeeded along that path, it is doubtful that he would have lived through the decades to come, much less finish his role as father to this writer! The loss of sailors on German submarines during World War II was indeed devastating.

Given his rejection by the military, his wish for an engineering education would involve attending the Technical University (Technische Hochschule, or TH) of Darmstadt. He could and did live at home, and fortunately, his relatives stepped in with financial help to allow that dream to be realized.

Sig's years at the TH Darmstadt were happy ones. One of the great loves he exercised beyond his studies was track and field, with an emphasis on long-distance running. (How the Reichsmarine found him to be physically inadequate will remain a mystery, but I am grateful they did.) Sig's studies focused on *Maschinenbau* (machine construction), what an English speaker today would call "mechanical engineering." His years at the TH involved a mandatory practicum whereby "engineering" experience was gained by doing something practical. In his case, he spent a summer minding the propulsion system of a steam-powered barge, where his learning also involved shoveling a lot of coal. He told of happy times on that adventure, often shirtless on the barge deck as it cruised the rivers and canals of the country. He kept detailed records of boiler parameters, coal usage, and similar engineering data. The shoveling probably improved his upper-body physique. It was a good summer. Closer to academic utility was a later time spent as a Praktikant (a required internship in the industry for certification as an engineer) working for the Deutsche Reichsbahn, the national railway, on the maintenance of steam locomotives. Perhaps that is where my love for trains originated, genetically speaking!

The curriculum at the TH involved five years of study and yielded a "Diplom Ingenieur" certificate that is recognized in the United States as equivalent to a master's degree. Sig was always proud of that accomplishment and never failed to note that he was a "Dipl. Ing.," even in the United States, where the significance of the title is not generally appreciated. His 1936 graduation certification, like that from the Gymnasium, is full of stamps and fancy signatures and goes on to note outstanding academic performance, along with a note that the person concerned did regular physical exercises.

It is during this time at the TH that Sig made many friends that he kept over the years. He also met Else Rahn at a small party a friend gave for her daughter and some of the members of the Allgemeine Sports Club, where Sig was a member. This club was a community of sports enthusiasts. He called the club a "fraternity" and as such had little commonality with members living together as a community, as is customary in an American academic fraternity. He was to encounter that concept a little later in life.

Little is recorded of Sig's courtship with Else. At the time, she was a working nurse at a hospital in Schotten some 100 km (70 miles) from Darmstatdt, that he covered, starry-eyed, numerous times on a bicycle to be with her. According to Google, that ride would have taken five hours and eleven minutes on today's bike paths. A year of romance led to their marriage in 1937. As was, and remains, customary, the marriage was first done in a civil ceremony, followed by a religious one in a beautiful chapel on the Neckar River.

Sig had just started employment after graduation at the Junkers Werke Alten. The tradition in German industry at that time was to take on new employees in training programs to see where they might fit into the organization or where their interests might lead them. As a new mechanical engineer, I am sure he looked forward to working in an arena where mechanical things reign supreme: engines. At the time, Junkers was fabricating powerful aircraft piston engines. His first assignment was to help design a means to augment the engine power by manipulating the exhaust stream for additional thrust on the Jumo (Junkers Motors) 210 and 211 engines. For the connoisseur, these engines are inverted (crank shaft above the piston heads) V-12 piston engines. This work involved flight testing and flying, which he thoroughly enjoyed! The improvements made to the engines resulted in a speed record flight of a Ju 87 airplane. A subsequent assignment, still having to do with piston engines, was investigating two-stroke, opposed-piston diesel engines (Jumo 205), wherein there are no cylinder heads but rather two crankshafts, each connected to pairs of pistons moving toward one another to compress air. The engine was the first and one of very few successful diesel engines in the aviation service. In these tasks, he learned the fundamentals of power interactions with gas flows, a skill that would serve him well when the time came to address the challenges of operating a jet engine.

It is hard to discern from the Family Book how Sig felt about leaving his mother and sister in Darmstadt and moving 280 miles away to Dessau, but I assume his new wife made all the difference. It was a day's train journey away, and the trains did run efficiently. The work was a great draw. In Dessau, Sig would make his deepest connections with other German aircraft engine engineers.

Aerial view of the Junkers facility in Dessau taken before the war

It is also difficult to know the character of one's father at the social level before one's birth and even later as a child growing up under his roof. In Sig's case, the matter is made more difficult because the events to follow as our family navigated through World War II had a significant emotional impact on his Weltanschauung. A son cannot realistically see past such events to see clearly the man that his father was. What does appear to be true is that he was always polite and pleasant to all people around him. Meeting his acquaintances, even in later years, always left me an impression of their having had very pleasant interactions. The other side of that coin is that he hid a lot of stress. That was manifested in occasional expressions of impatience and intolerance within the family setting.

At home, and only there, as far as I can tell, did he allow his frustrations in life to rise to the surface, and when things did not go his way, a darkness befell him that the family had to endure. Fixing things his way was expected, much to the apprehension of his children. These impressions arise here because the woman he married played a challenging but effective role in defusing problematic issues and softening such times with calm. She fulfilled this role with kindness and aplomb, in war and later in peace, when I could watch it firsthand as an adult.

CHAPTER 9

Partnership for a New Life

Who was the woman who became Sig's wife? Else Rahn was a nurse. She was orphaned early in life. In 1910, at age five, she lost her mother. She remembered little of her, save for her pained face as she lay dying. At eight years old, she lost her father. He was a mechanic and court locksmith with a shop in the back of the house, with the front rented out. She vaguely remembered her father working on bicycles, as a small business out of the house. She remembered going on short journeys, sitting on a special bicycle seat behind him.

Her parents were in what was called a "mixed" marriage, consisting of a Protestant father and a Catholic mother, or the other way around. It hardly matters. What did matter is that because she was of a "mixed" marriage, neither side was willing to take her in after her father died. At that time, her father's mother (her paternal grandmother) was living in the household, and the two of them were eventually taken in by the family of an aunt, where they were seen as somewhat of a burden—such was the modicum of family life for Else.

Misfortune continued to follow Else. When she was seventeen, her aunt died and she was once again alone and forced to find a place in the world for herself. She was ultimately "encouraged" by whoever remained in her reduced family to attend a nursing school to learn the trade. The period of her training saw her as a ward of a distant family member, perhaps the person who encouraged her to study nursing, from whom she also learned the culinary arts. She did learn this skill well, as I can attest! She had studied and worked as a nurse for about a decade when she met Sig and they hit it off, even though she was seven years older than him. By then, she had enjoyed her nursing work, which included a number of trainings, notably in the growing field of x-rays. She would come to rely on nursing again as events of the war came to pass.

Else and Siegfried settled in Dessau in the state of Sachsen-Anhalt, because of the location of Sig's work at Junkers aircraft. The city is about 70 miles southwest of Berlin on the Elbe River. The general area is a floodplain of the Elbe, with Dessau on the west shore of the river. One of the region's attributes is the church in nearby Wittenberg, where Martin Luther nailed his Ninety-Five Theses on the church door and started the Reformation. Dessau was rather small in size, with light industry consisting of a sugar refinery and a brewery. A significant impact on this sleepy town was the Junkers aircraft and motor facilities, a major industrial enterprise.

There were other small local enterprises, but Dessau's claim to worldwide recognition was the Bauhaus. It was an empty set of buildings then. Today, they are again in their originally intended usage. The Bauhaus was an architectural and artistic movement formed by an assortment of modern free-thinking artists and builders to exercise free thoughts on modern life. The movement started in the early 1920s in Berlin, moved to Weimar, and finally landed in Dessau, in part thanks to Hugo Junkers. The moves to the various cities were precipitated by the economic difficulties of the 1920s. These were dominated by runaway inflation and the associated political turmoil. The cities involved where the Bauhaus settled were expected to play financial supporting roles. In the end, political volatility determined where discretionary spending from community funds was available and directed—until it was not.

The Bauhaus was located in Dessau when the Nazi government took over Germany. The Nazis had no use for free-thinking artists. In 1933, the Bauhaus was disbanded, and the principals and their students were scattered around the world. The director, Walter Gropius, went to the United States and taught at Harvard University, and others went to the University of Chicago to do the same thing. These individuals nurtured an important cadre of architects in the American postwar years.

During the time of the Bauhaus, Dessau had allowed the building of a set of experimental dwelling units for individuals from all over Europe

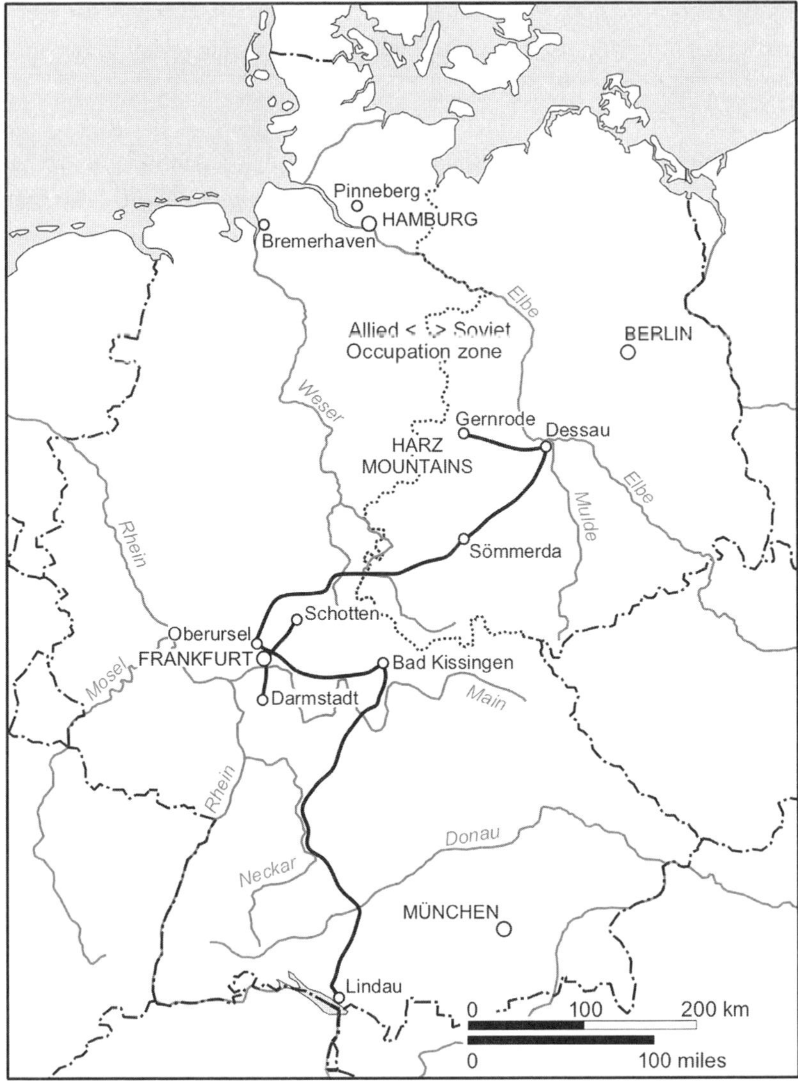

Germany (ca. 1945), showing locations of residences and (*dotted*) the Soviet Occupation Zone boundary. *Andreas Illert*

and local residents to ply their art. These buildings reflected the modern thinking in architecture that was a centerpiece of the movement. In addition to architecture, the traditional art forms were pursued, notably textiles, ceramics, and furniture design. The buildings were later occupied by the incoming Nazi government for unknown purposes. Most were spared the bombing of the city, and they largely remain today as a tribute to heady and hopeful times.

Another new set of residences were built later in the mid-1930s across the street from the Bauhaus, which was, by then, empty of artists. This is where Sig and Mutti settled. (Else was not yet a "Mutti," but that was about to change in August 1939 when I arrived.) The address was then "Schlageterplatz," named after a Nazi honoree of dubious renown. That feature made it challenging to locate the place after the war, as the Communist government of the Deutsche Demokratische Republik (DDR) would not likely have maintained the Nazi street name. On a visit after the fall of the wall, the author and other family members sought to find the address. We had to resort to finding and asking an "old" person for possible directions because young people would have not known the old street name, eliminated fifty years earlier. To our pleasant surprise, the name is now "Bauhausplatz."

The DDR occupied a large chunk of Germany that, for Sig as well as me, was too scary to visit after the war. This fear was justified by the well-documented attempts at Republikflucht (flight from the republic) that often ended badly, with escapees shot by guards at the border wall. With human ingenuity being what it is, however, some people did successfully escape by spectacular means, as documented in a Berlin museum dedicated to such feats. Further fuel for concern was that Sig's departure from the Soviet Occupation Zone that became the DDR involved terms that were not ideal from the Soviet perspective. But let's not leap ahead in our story.

The prewar and early war, times were happy for my parents. Sig was doing the work he loved, developing the supercharging of piston aircraft engines. In very short order, his experience and the handling of that assignment led him to be invited to join the Franz group of engineers concerned with a new type of aircraft propulsion engine, the jet engine.

CHAPTER 10

The End of Summer

I was born a few days before the first flight of a jet-powered airplane. The war clouds were on the horizon, and within a week, Hitler invaded Poland and thereby liberated the devil by opening the gates of hell.

Mutti reminisced that for Germans, the time was not unhappy. The war was far away, and she was very happy being a new mother. The propaganda machine was doling out good news, and the war was not directly impacting the civilian population. There was no political stress because newspapers and public discourse that might have questioned the good government news were silent or silenced. Shortages, rations, and depravity were still in the future.

Father and son (author), 1940

Sig dug into his work on a new type of jet engine. After all, the basic idea was that the jet engine was a way to overcome the limitation imposed by the movement of pistons in cylinders of ordinary engines, by allowing the new jet engine to radically increase the amount of air through an engine. The idea was simple: more air, more fuel, more power. Secondarily, the use of a jet engine overcomes the fundamental speed limit imposed on the airplane by its use of a propeller. That intrigued the military powers on both sides of the new conflict.

The story of the Jumo engine that would power the first German jet fighter in service is a tale of hurry and shortage of resources. The first run of an engine was a little more than a year (October 1940) after the contract award in July 1939. Before 1941 ended, the program succeeded with maximum thrust and ten-hour run demonstrations. The first flight in a Messerschmitt Me 262, one of its designated airplanes, occurred in August 1942. By this time, the war was beginning to make demands on the economy that impacted the construction of the engine; shortages of the materials necessary began to impede progress. For example, alloying metals to make turbine blades so that the turbine can run as hot as possible were not available. Instead, the engineers had to make do with blade coatings. These were less than satisfactory because they did not hold up for very

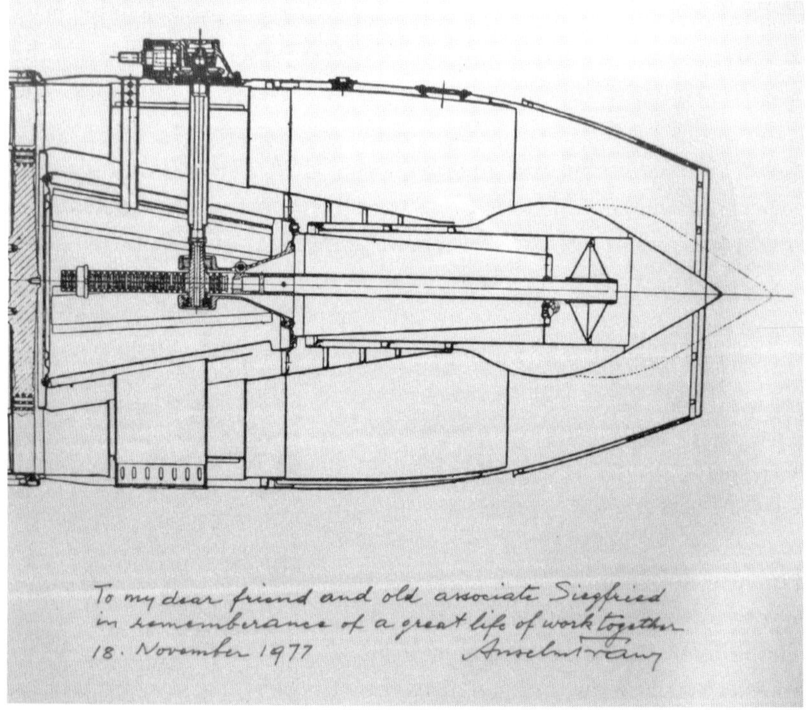

Cross section of the nozzle end of a Jumo 004 (*top*). The "onion" is the movable body that varies the flow through the exhaust nozzle on the right (in the center of the exhaust nozzle). The dotted onion shows its extreme position. Photo is of the control mechanism of a sectioned engine display at the National Museum of the United States Air Force.

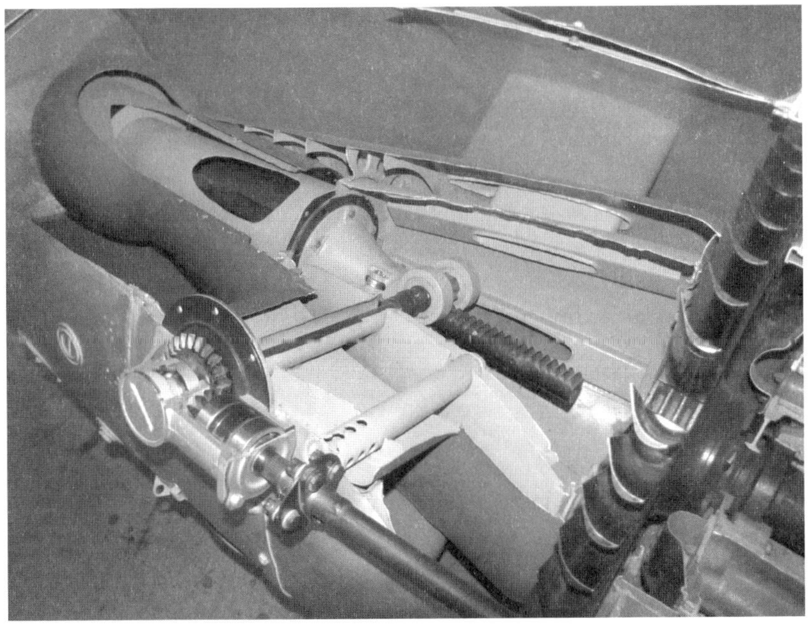

long. To the good, these engineers also had to develop air cooling techniques using relatively cool compressor air, a technology that was to see wide application in all engines that followed, even to this day.

The axial flow compressor engine has a built-in Achilles heel—at least it does if one does not recognize and deal with it. That complexity is that the compressor is built with a series of moving and stationary blades. The airflow relative to these blades must be oriented just right within a narrow angle range to allow the compressor as a whole to function well. In the case of the Jumo 004, the solution was to incorporate into the design, a modification of the exhaust nozzle that can modulate the airflow rate through the engine. Controlling the airflow rate was critical to maintaining the compressor blading flow to be efficient. More importantly, one had to avoid stall, which would render the engine nonfunctional. If such a stall were to occur in a military airplane as a result of rapid changes in power demand, the situation for the pilot would quickly degenerate to a dangerous state. Finally, the matter of the engine control had to be automated so that the pilot is not burdened by having to deal with its behavior. The design and implementation of such a control system was the task assigned to and achieved by Sig Decher.

Sig's design consisted of a mechanical system that uses the measurement of airflow rate and engine RPM to drive a center body in the nozzle. The mechanism adjusts the airflow rate through the engine to be correct, without attention from the pilot of the airplane. The center-body was humorously called the "onion" by the engineers. This design fixed the issue and allowed Sig to apply for a patent to cover his invention in Germany and, after the war, in the United States. He was notified by the Junkers patent office that the patent for the axial flow compressor control system (Axialverdichter Fühlsteurung/1764) applied for on March 11, 1942, was granted on May 25, 1944. The American patent was granted in 1954. In Germany, the successful patent award yielded Sig a monetary sum of 50 Reichsmarks. The Reichsmark was the currency in Germany from 1924 until 1948. To scale the value of the award, we noted that his salary at the time was 350 Reichsmarks per month.

The War

The history of the military use of the Me 262 by the Luftwaffe is interesting. The airplane and its engines did not become available for military service until the summer of 1944, and two historical aspects of that airplane are important. First, there was the anticipated invasion of the Nazi-occupied mainland of Europe, which Hitler called "Fortress Europe." The German military did not know where or when the invasion (attempt) was to take place. The landings were ultimately made in Normandy in early June 1944. A German defensive position thus had to be flexible and capable of rapid response. Military leaders at the Luftwaffe had determined that the fast jet fighter, faster than any piston engine-powered aircraft by a healthy 100 miles per hour, was best used as a fighter to thwart the Allied bombing of cities and industrial targets. An argument with military leaders not to use the airplane in this way was initially won by Hitler, who forbade the use of the Me 262 as a fighter. He wanted it used as a fast bomber to delay the invasion forces wherever they landed, until such time as land forces could be mustered to push the Allies back into the sea.

The second aspect was that the successful bombing by the Allies concentrating on fuel production facilities effectively caused Germany to run out of gas. The fuel necessary for running an army and an air force was becoming severely limited. By the end of summer 1944, Hitler gave in to allow the Me 262 to be used as an interceptor to engage the English Lancasters at night and the American Boeing B-17s by day together with their escort fighters, but it was too late. The tide of war had changed with the Normandy invasion and the liberation of Paris. During the winter of 1945, the Allies had fought and won the last major battle with the German army and were ready to cross the Rhine River. German participation in jet aviation was effectively over because Allied air power dominated the German skies.

It would be a false impression if one concluded that the German effort at jet engine development was singular. The British, under the leadership of Frank Whittle, and the Americans through a shared involvement between General Electric and Rolls-Royce, were also hard at work on a parallel effort. The details are well told elsewhere (see *Powering the World's Airliners*). They include the unsuccessful axial flow engine of Alan A. Griffith, flown in 1943. The British axial flow engine lacked the control system that shields a pilot from having to simultaneously fly an airplane and a compressor! Much more promising was the radial flow compressor engine pioneered by Whittle. Such an engine was easier to build and operate because it was significantly less prone to stalling. The first British flight of a jet engine was in 1942, using a single Whittle-engined Gloster E.28/39. Subsequently, the twin-engine Gloster Meteor fighter was built and deployed during the war, primarily over England, to shoot down the V-1 cruise missiles launched from German-occupied France. Even after the Allies liberated France and V-1 launch sites that were no longer available to the Germans, the Meteor continued its defense mission over England. German bombing by aircraft became less and less of a threat as the war wound down. Unfortunately, the German bombing terror on English cities switched to the V-2 long-range rocket launched from mobile sites deep inside Germany and still-occupied countries. It was so crudely guided as to be ineffective as a military weapon but randomly killed many civilians, primarily in London. But that is another story, though it involves the engineers who built the V-2 with a technology transfer to the United States known as "Operation Paperclip." This operation played a major role in shaping our family's future.

CHAPTER 12

Wartime Family Life

The summer of 1941 saw the first use of air raid preparations that included exercising sirens mounted on the roof of the Bauhaus. They were very loud and I apparently did not like the audio assault. Mutti had packed a suitcase with essentials for the possibility of the apartment being destroyed or unusable. That suitcase followed the family to every air raid and drill until 1945. We spent a number of nights in a shelter in the dubiously effective basement of the building, listening to distant rumbles and hoping to be spared. In all, it is estimated that there were about twenty air raids on the city.

During the spring of 1942, the family was enlarged with the arrival of my brother, Uli (formally Ulrich), which made Mutti's management of the family even more challenging. Mutti contrasts her stay at the hospital to the earlier one when I was involved as more somber. When I was born, the hospital provided flowers for her nine-day stay. Now, none of those simple pleasures were part of the event. The war had taken a toll on life. It seems there was little to be purchased in stores, especially what must have been thought as less than essential, such as the availability of flowers. The months thereafter saw critical health issues for my brother. For about four months, he was placed in a clinic because he failed to gain weight. The reason puzzled the doctors. It is hard to say what role the scarcity of food and medicines played in this episode, which was devolving badly. My parents were called in twice to see him for one last time. Fortunately, he recovered for no reason that anyone could identify. He had to do a lot of healing, which included emotionally reattaching to his mother upon returning home. In spite of the increasingly difficult times,

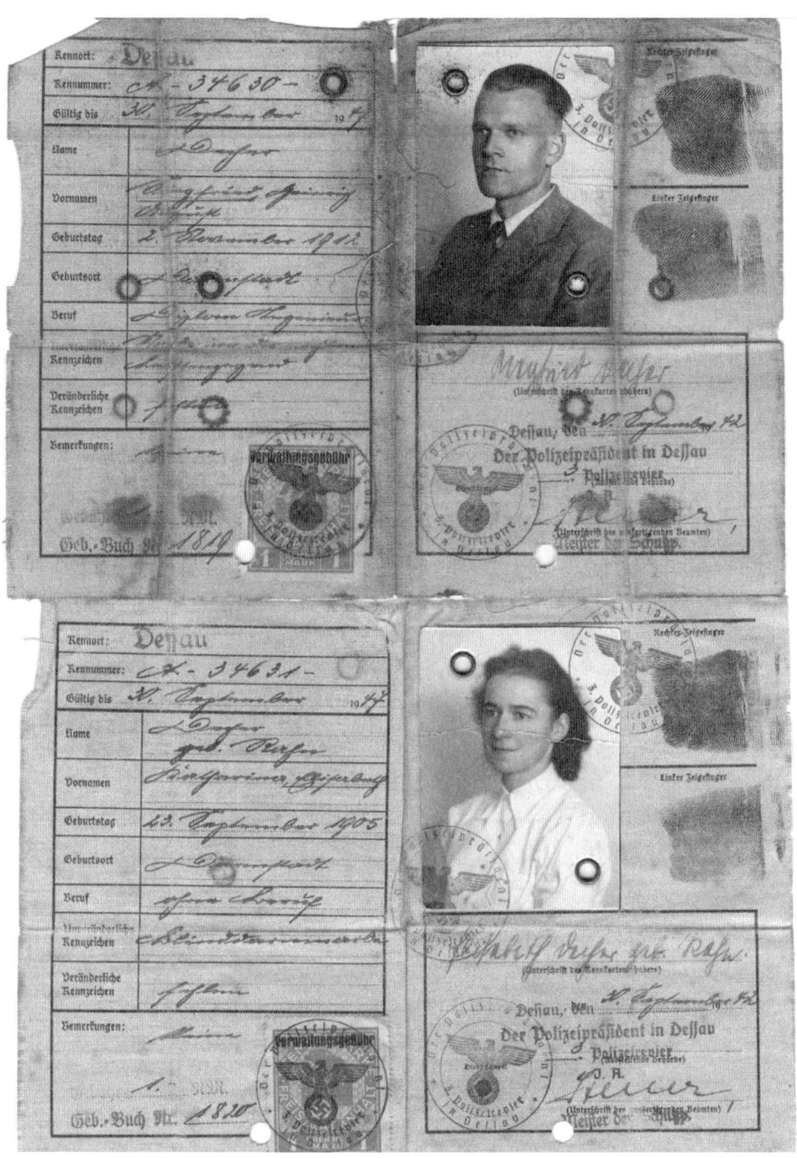

Kennort: Dessau
Kennummer: A - 34630 -
Gültig bis 30. September 1947
Name
Vornamen
Geburtstag 2. Dezember 1912
Geburtsort
Beruf
Unveränderliche Kennzeichen
Veränderliche Kennzeichen
Bemerkungen:
Geb.-Buch Nr. 1819
Verwaltungsgebühr
Rechter Zeigefinger
Linker Zeigefinger
(Unterschrift des Kennkarteninhabers)
Dessau, den 30. September 42
Der Polizeipräsident in Dessau
Polizeirevier
(Unterschrift des ausfertigenden Beamten)

Kennort: Dessau
Kennummer: A - 34631 -
Gültig bis 30. September 1947
Name
Vornamen
Geburtstag 23. September 1905
Geburtsort
Beruf
Unveränderliche Kennzeichen
Veränderliche Kennzeichen
Bemerkungen:
Geb.-Buch Nr. 1820
Verwaltungsgebühr
Rechter Zeigefinger
Linker Zeigefinger
(Unterschrift des Kennkarteninhabers)
Dessau, den 30. September 42
Der Polizeipräsident in Dessau
Polizeirevier
(Unterschrift des ausfertigenden Beamten)

The 1942 identification papers that German citizens had to carry at all times. Sig (*top*) and his wife, Else (*bottom*).

his health returned to normal. At that point, the war was having a major impact on civilian life.

In 1942, Germany was a well-controlled state where everything about everyone was meticulously known and cataloged. Every person had to carry identification papers at all times that looked something like the one pictured opposite, dated in that year.

Considering the wartime environment, the development of the Jumo 004 was going pretty well. In 1943, Sig became one of the principals of the engine development team, with a promotion to "section chief." It is also likely that this was the time when Anselm Franz took over management of the new project bureau, specifically the Jumo 004, then headed by Otto Mader. Mader had become ill with leukemia and died the following year. In that same year, Sig was awarded a War Service recognition award. In his files is a document pictured below that was probably mailed to him at Junkers. Generally speaking, such a document would be difficult to preserve, especially in the times that followed the war, because it might imply a relation with Nazi officialdom or an attitude toward Nazism that might not or did not exist. Nevertheless, as the writer of these words, I am glad this document was saved because it surely serves to call attention to the importance of the jet engine work Sig and his colleagues were doing. That work kept him out of having to serve in the Wehrmacht. From a personal viewpoint, this recognition was critical to his survival because it was given at the time of German setbacks suffered on the Eastern Front. The Battle of Stalingrad had just been lost a few months before, initiating the German retreat from Russia. The defeat became the turning point of the war.

From the perspective of time gone by, it seems a valid concern as to whether a person would have to have been a Nazi Party member to receive such an award. Sig never talked about that, except to curtly state that he was never a member. As we will see, he will make a case for that being true to the Allies, and they took him at his word. The records also show that the promotion doubled his salary, for a while anyway, because fortune was less and less inclined to smile upon Germany.

Prior to this time, work in an engineering office or factory was what could be termed normal, except for the pressure brought on by official agencies. There were war-imposed limitations in how the work was done. It might have been impossible to obtain this or that or do something that

Jm Namen
des
Deutschen Volkes
verleihe ich

dem Unterabteilungsleiter
Siegfried D e c h e r
Dessau

das Kriegsverdienstkreuz
2. Klasse

Berlin, den 2. Juni 1943

Der Führer

The War Merit Cross Certificate, Second Class, signed quite likely by Hitler, among others. The certificate states "In the Name of the German people, I hereby award to Subsection Chief, Siegfried Decher of Dessau the War Merit Cross, Second Class, Berlin, 2 June 1943. The Führer."

would have been more readily doable in a peacetime setting. There were lots of late hours spent in the office, and there were no computers to help with the work. Sig's old slide rule shows that it was well used. While family photo albums contained many pictures until 1942–43, there is a void of such documentation later. The time was not to be remembered in pictures. The opportunities to spend a weekend in the forest or some other nice place had vanished, along with access to film for the camera.

The records in our possession show no evidence of the working conditions in the Junkers factory. At some war production facilities, postwar headlines revealed horrid conditions: slave and forced labor, and worse. The extent to which these aspects of wartime production were present, or known to the engineers, is at best a guess. What is clear, however, is that the stress on successfully building the jet engines was immense, and Sig may have internalized a lot of it, only to have it reappear later in life as a heart condition that killed him at a relatively early age of sixty-seven. This is what Mutti, the nurse, thought or surmised.

The times for the civilian engineers became particularly difficult as the tide of war changed. Their work had to proceed quickly to a successful end, or else. At worst, the "or else" included the ever-present threat of conscription into the Wehrmacht in a horrible and possibly short future.

Whatever normal might have looked like, it vanished when the bombing began. The first of a number of evacuations from the city to the countryside took place in December 1943.

During the summer of 1944, the Allies focused their bombing to a large degree on industrial and fuel production targets. That campaign was indeed very successful in thwarting German military activity for lack of fuel for trucks, tanks, and aircraft. Additionally, the increasing bombing threat on cities was worrisome enough to cause Sig and Mutti, together with several other families working at Junkers, to move their families out of the city. For us, the move was to a farm in Bavaria in the summer of 1944. There, life was relatively peaceful, but the impact of the war was very much felt. There may have been little fear of bombing events, but there were increasing shortages of stuffs like sugar, flour, dairy products, coffee, and similar commodities that are produced on an industrial scale or had historically been imported. Fortunately, farm life provided some basic necessities like eggs, poultry, and garden vegetables, especially in the summertime. The absence of German men, who were now at the front, meant that prisoners of war had to be used to help with farmwork. From Mutti's story, several Russians labored around the farm, and I am told, as a five-year-old, I enjoyed interacting with them while they worked. They likely missed their own children back in Russia.

At the end of the summer of 1944, several of the Junkers engineer families were moved to Gernrode in the Harz mountains, while the fathers stayed at work in Dessau. Gernrode was a small town, about 60 miles to the west of Dessau. It was a place where one was less likely to have to deal with bombings. Still, while the mothers were bicycling around looking for potatoes that had been left in fields, there were occasional encounters with British Hurricane fighter aircraft, which shot at everyone and everything that moved. One time, the mothers did successfully avoid becoming targets by dumping their bicycles and taking shelter behind trees. Their daily searches were for anything that might be edible. On the list of necessary activities were long walks along the narrow-gauge tracks of the local railroad, looking for chunks of coal that might have been dropped by the steam locomotives. They were used for cooking, complementing the wood gathered in the forest.

The times were rough. A number of the children in our circle, including the author, contracted scarlet fever. In the larger community, store shelves were empty. Sharing was not often done because people feared that whatever was in the cellar or cupboard would be needed at some time in their uncertain future. Some rations were distributed during these hard times, specifically to families with young children. One day, a neighbor's cat ate our family's butter ration for the month—a half pound of butter disappeared from the kitchen table! To add insult to injury, it repaid the pleasure by getting thoroughly sick. That was not a happy moment! Another happy family memory Mutti conveyed was that, at the time, newspapers had to be cut up for toilet purposes. No toilet paper was available to be hoarded! Surely the newspapers used for that purpose had to have been a Nazi propaganda tool, and what an appropriate use for them!

Mutti reported that in the first of the two places we occupied in Gernrode, the owners, who had to accommodate refugees and others by order of the town management, took to stealing from our own meager milk rations. That episode led to a move to another house in the town where people were friendlier. The Eggers family lived in the same house. Sig and Gerhard Eggers took time from work on a couple of occasions and bicycled the 60 miles to visit us in Gernrode.

During the Dessau years, after my brother's birth, Mutti had the help of an eighteen-year-old girl named Elli, who was associated with the family as a mother's assistant. She accompanied us to Gernrode and did what she could to help. The flood of refugees from the Eastern Front, where the Soviet army was advancing, was immense. The people were German speakers from East Prussia, Silesia, and even from a part of the Soviet Union where Germans were encouraged to settle during the time of Catherine the Great, who reigned in Russia in the last third of the eighteenth century. The tales of rape, murder, and mayhem brought westward with the refugees were a source of panic among civilians. Elli pleaded to stay connected with our family. Whether the American authorities would have allowed her to be a part of the family was a question that our parents worried about in the months to come, needlessly however, because Mutti sent Elli to Dessau on a bicycle to retrieve a bag of potatoes. She never returned, and we ultimately lost contact with this loved and appreciated young girl.

To obtain a realistic picture of this time for German civilians facing the Russian advance on Berlin in 1945, the reader is directed to a appendix 3 for a short story that vividly paints a picture of terror and misery. The connection to the author's family history is established much later in circumstances that are fortuitous and happy. Specifically, in 1982, the author and his family spent a sabbatical year at the University of Karlsruhe in Germany where he met several Germans who were either in the war or born after it to parents profoundly affected by the wartime events. One was a young man whose mother narrates the story told in the appendix. Hers is just one of many horrific stories. The other heart wrenching encounter is with a former soldier who fought in the Monte Cassino battle of the Italian Campaign of World War II. He was gravely injured there and narrowly survived the ordeal. The stories drawn from these encounters, the first by means of the written words you can read and the second from the shared stories are that people's spirit can, amazingly, thrive in spite of their experiences. Such experiences are testaments to the resilience of the human spirit when it encounters war. As a matter of related interest, the author edited a memoir (see Doughty in the bibliography) by an American intelligence officer who also fought in Italy in World War II cementing a profound appreciation of what that part of the war was like for soldiers on both sides. The reader may or may not wish to interrupt this story with a trip to the appendix, so we return to our present journey.

The fall and winter of 1944–45 was a hellishly bad time for much of Germany because the bombing was relentless. In September, Darmstadt, my parents' hometown, was, in Mutti's words, "bombed flat." Fortunately, the apartment where Sig's mother and sister Annemarie lived was spared. Annemarie made unsuccessful attempts at contacting Sig to assure him that the family was alright. These attempts included trying to go to the post office, where a functional telephone might be found, but the journeys were overwhelming. Nothing worked. There was no electricity, no telephone, no post office, and the water supply was problematic. Everything was thoroughly broken, including hope, most of all. Annemarie tells of navigating the utterly destroyed and almost unrecognizable streets, stepping over the bodies of people who were caught outside air raid shelters and were killed by the detonations of bombs exploding nearby and random shrapnel. The city of Dresden was firebombed one February night and reduced to ashes. Dresden, the "Venice of the North," was no more. In that phase of the war, the bombing destruction bordered on pointless. The German V-1 Buzz Bombs and later V-2 ballistic missile attacks on London in particular also qualified as pointless from a military viewpoint, especially since Germany was in a military full-scale retreat with a bad ending in plain sight for those who chose to see it. In general, the military value of targeting civilians seems often to be, in retrospect, very small. That is not to state that such bombing can never be effective. The atomic bombing of Japan certainly argues that point.

The reader might appreciate a story of the Dresdner Frauenkirche (Our Lady's Church), destroyed on February 13, 1945, now reconstructed, and reconsecrated after resting many years in the former DDR as a pile of numbered stones. It was and is again a cathedral of enormous cultural significance to Germany. The story, ending with a golden cross on the tower donated by the British Crown, is a story onto itself.

Dessau was bombed in March, and again we were luckier than many in that our place was spared. Working conditions at Junkers had become unmanageable. The air raids on Dessau damaged the

Otto Mader building where the Jumo 004 project was centered, so that the work had to be dispersed to a number of sites around town. Work was, for the engineers involved, technically and physically challenging. They could not work together in a conventional office setting. Franz's people were moved to, among other places, a house in the city's nearby forest, the attic of a home for old ladies where undergarments were often hung to dry after washing, a small factory on the outskirts of town, and other places. Franz and others had to bicycle between these locations in order to coordinate whatever had to be done. There were few cars available.

Speaking of cars, the engineers building jet engines probably had access to cars, as most private cars had been confiscated and repurposed for military needs. For getting around during the last months of the war, cars were one thing. Quite another was gasoline. There was little to be had. Clever people managed something of a workaround to that problem. Since wood (and sometimes coal) was more abundant, they devised a contraption consisting of a closed container into which the solid fuel could be heated with an open fire under it. The temperature of the container had to be sufficiently high so that volatiles (and carbon monoxide) were emitted from the solids inside. The resulting noxious and poisonous gas was led, via piping, to the carburetor of the automobile engine, where it was put to work. The engine produced a little power, albeit barely. The open fire in the car, the space taken up by the gas generator, keeping a stack of wood on board, and feeding the fire was awkward, to put it mildly. Nevertheless, a modicum of transport was possible for desperate circumstances. My friend Karsten reports that this modality, in a small delivery truck form, was used after the war (near the end of June 1945) to get him and his family from their residence in Dessau to a waiting C-47 at the airport in nearby Quedlinburg for the evacuation to Hamburg in the British Occupation Zone. The air trip was short, serving as a quick escape to a western zone. The rest of the trip was by truck. His father, like Sig, was on the Operation Paperclip list.

The nearby quaint little medieval town of Quedlinburg was badly damaged in yet another raid that was finally the impetus for Sig to join the family in Gernrode. Transportation to Gernrode consisted of hitchhiking; his bicycle was stolen or wrecked and so were the train tracks and train service. He made it, although in a sorry state with what might

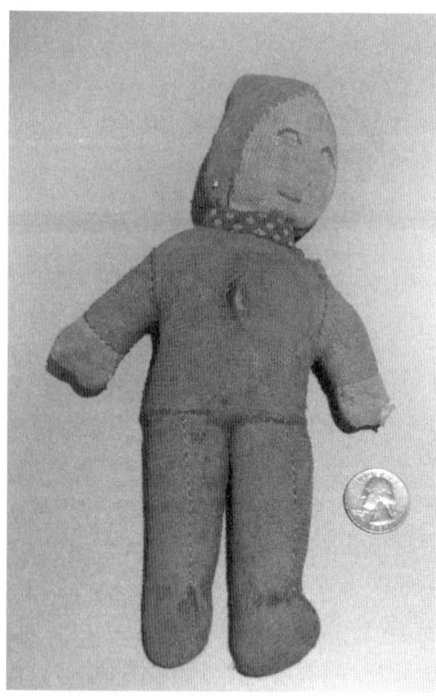

"Puppi," my bomb shelter comfort doll

have been pneumonia or tuberculosis. An accurate diagnosis was not available but mercifully it was not TB. That forced him to spend some time recovering to a minimally functioning state of health and this at a time when antibiotics were not available, certainly in Germany. Even in Gernrode, people feared the possibility of air raids. When the alarms sounded, the threats were usually overflights to other places, but one never knew. Nevertheless, our parents usually grabbed the barest necessities and their ready-to-go suitcase, stuck them with Uli into a baby carriage, and hurried us into the nearby woods. These were thought to be relatively safe, though usually without shelter and cold. I had with me, then as always, a little soft, stuffed doll from which I gained a modicum of comfort—or was it the other way around? It was about 10 inches tall, red in color save for its face and feet, and with a red cap. I still have this doll thanks to Mutti having saved it. Its name was Puppi, whose pronunciation amused my American-speaking wife, Mary, as it is neither "puppy" nor "poopy"!

We stayed in the woods until the all-clear siren sounded and allowed for a return to normal life, as it were... to await the next wail of sirens.

The bombing campaign of the winter was terror on a massive scale. For the Allies to believe that it might cause Nazi officialdom in Berlin to consider a process leading to peace seems absurd, but then, that is war. The affected civilians were hardly in a position to influence the course of war in any way. Yes, there would be Nazi fanatics in the population, and it would be good to take them out of action, but most of the people had other concerns. The stressed-out and semidelirious Nazi "government," if that is what the collection of fanatics in Berlin can be called, were dealing with the demand for unconditional surrender. No one, least of all Hitler, was ready for anything close to that course of action. He was willing to die a "hero's" death and was willing to take everyone else with him. The Nazi high command had learned of the Allied plans for partition and occupation. Nazi spies had secured that information as postwar details had been decided by the Allies at the Yalta Conference in February 1945.

For the local residents, the coming moves by the Russian army to the east and the American army in the west were not yet clear. They probably did not know that the region near Dessau was going to be turned over to the Soviet Union as their occupation sector. All they knew was that the Russians were coming. That first week in May 1945 was a strange time for Germans in our general area. A few could assess the situation well enough to take in the bigger picture: the American army stopped fighting and was not moving, but the war was not concluded. Berlin was still in Nazi hands. The US general Eisenhower's idea was to let the Soviets conquer Berlin. This was much to the annoyance of British prime minister Winston Churchill, who feared, and rightly as it turned out, that it gave the Russians a firm foothold in Germany and eastern Europe, where they ultimately drew an "Iron Curtain" around their "possessions." No matter for now, however, the modern Thirty Years' War ended with another bullet shot in the Berlin bunker. In another week or so, it would be May 8, 1945, and VE-day.

The larger picture was that major parts of the provinces of Thüringen and Sachsen-Anhalt were conquered and occupied by the US Army. Tensions between the United States and the Soviet Union were already making an appearance in diplomatic circles, and these tensions were felt by the military commanders, General Eisenhower specifically. It was his decision to halt the advance of Western Allied troops on the Elbe River. This river, together with its Mulde tributary, cut a diagonal line across eastern Germany. Eisenhower's thinking was that there was little point in expending resources and losing American lives to conquer territory that would ultimately be turned over to the Soviets. Further, there was also a risk to be mitigated to have American and Soviet troops fire upon one another as they squeezed whatever German units were between them into submission.

Our family's great fortune was that Dessau lies on the west shore of the Elbe River. Our first contact with Allied forces would be with the US Army. People on the other side of the river would not have the opportunity to be conquered and processed by Americans. For me, it is hard to imagine what our lives behind the Iron Curtain might have been like.

In those last weeks of the war, the uncertainty about Soviet troops was felt by everyone. My mother, in her searches for food and wood fuel for cooking, found a discarded military handgun. It had probably belonged to a German soldier who was fleeing from the advancing Soviet troops. She resolved to do the family in if and when the Russians came to take over and bad things were to happen. Father had learned of the US Army's imposition of martial law, where a civilian's possession of a weapon was sufficient reason to be shot. He would not have the gun around and saw to its disappearance.

Our encounters with retreating German troops at times turned out to be beneficial, occasionally, because Mutti once managed to obtain a large piece of ham and cigarettes that could be traded for food. It was a new world.

The peace that was to come with VE-day was preceded by an event about nine months earlier on July 20, 1944, that could be termed as potentially fateful for the course of the war. On that day, there was an assassination attempt on Hitler by people who had organized a new government-in-waiting to take the place of the Nazis after Hitler was dead. They might have negotiated a very different end to the war and would surely have altered the course of history, along with the lives of the people in our story. Yet the question of "How?" is impossible to answer. Hitler's survival and reaction did not turn out well for the brave Germans who made the unsuccessful attempt. They suffered indescribably cruel ends. A very personal story of the people involved is told by Christabel Bielenberg in her book *When I Was German, 1934–1945: An English Woman in Nazi Germany*.

CHAPTER 13

Peace and Occupation Uncertainties

The last of the war in Gernrode was an artillery barrage on the nineteenth of April. We, together with others living in the building, had to take shelter in the basement of the brewery next to our home. The next day, American troops marched into town with jubilant Germans lining the roads. The jubilation was a mixture of liberation from fear and violence and apprehension, as the American army was the enemy in whose hands the German population found itself. On April 21, we heard that they took Dessau.

The Allied march into Germany involved stilling military opposition and securing the cities and towns so that no further military action was possible. In a small town like Gernrode, this amounted to Americans occupying the *Rathaus* (town hall, literally "Council House") and identifying who was who and what resources were available to allow a controlled peace to reign. Specifically, criminals had to be identified and held. Thus a contingent of soldiers was put in place.

The US Army, as a member of the Allies, had military attachés from other Allies embedded in its command. In our area, the attachés were Russian, because they were to take the area over at a later date when hostilities ceased altogether. The Russians also realized, of course, that they were dealing with technical resources, the German engineers, and were keen not to miss out on any future advantages that the captured Germans might bring. The Americans, for their part, were quite obliging

The residence building (*right*) in Gernrode where the Decher and Eggers families resided during the spring of 1945. The photo was taken in 2008. The clock factory on left was a brewery at the time, and its cellar served as a bomb shelter for the families and others. *Courtesy K. Eggers*

in that they did not keep the information about the German engineers a secret from the Russians.

The first more intimate contact with the Amis, as American troops were called by Germans, was with soldiers whose task it was to reduce the mass migration to the west. To that end, everyone was issued papers stating in which town they were to stay, whether they lived there or not, under threat of arrest if caught elsewhere. Sig and our family were in Gernrode at the time, and so their papers reflected that location. He convinced the American authorities that his proper residence was in Dessau, and thus the permanent residence of Dessau was noted on the identification papers issued by the US Army. With that established, the Americans became aware that a number of families in Gernrode were those of members of the engineering team from Junkers in Dessau. The next order of business was to get the various families in Gernrode back to Dessau. How this was accomplished is not in the records, but we were relocated back to our apartment across from the Bauhaus. In Dessau, the occupation forces could deal with the engineers as a group.

The next official contact was between the German engineers and American officers. The discussion centered on offers to be transported west before the American forces vacated the region for Soviet occupation. Such discussions were also held with a Soviet military attaché (to the Americans), who argued that staying in Dessau was the better course.

Sig's discussion with the Russians was interesting and partially documented in his correspondence with others. In short, there was considerable pressure to stay in Dessau and become part of a Russo-German joint development effort that continued and extended the Jumo 004 work. Housing and food were promised in abundance by stating that the engineers' status would entitle them to good treatment, as was the "tradition" in the Soviet communist system of rewards: "to each according to their contribution!" Naturally, there were German engineers leaning toward one side or the other, and the arguments were animated at times. Many believed that the Russian option could not be as bad as some imagined, and some just wanted to stay in the place where they had family connections or owned property.

Jumping ahead in history a little bit, Sig's correspondence made reference to two events that later reinforced his decision to go west as the better one. The first is that history will indeed reveal a sordid evolution of conditions in the Soviet Occupation Zone and the later German Democratic (hardly) Republic, abbreviated in German as the DDR. A

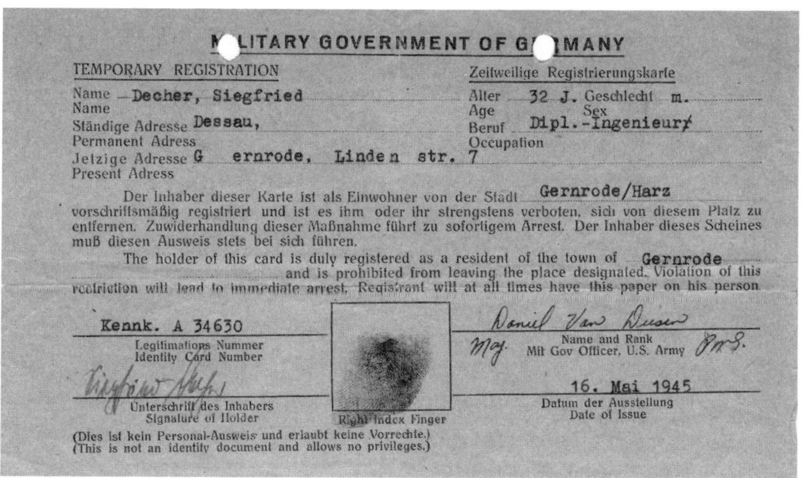

M LITARY GOVERNMENT OF G MANY

TEMPORARY REGISTRATION — Zeitweilige Registrierungskarte

Name / Name: Decher, Siegfried — Alter / Age: 32 J. — Geschlecht / Sex: m.

Ständige Adresse / Permanent Adress: Dessau, — Beruf / Occupation: Dipl.-Ingenieur

Jetzige Adresse / Present Adress: G ernrode, Linde n str. 7

Der Inhaber dieser Karte ist als Einwohner von der Stadt Gernrode/Harz vorschriftsmäßig registriert und ist es ihm oder ihr strengstens verboten, sich von diesem Platz zu entfernen. Zuwiderhandlung dieser Maßnahme führt zu sofortigem Arrest. Der Inhaber dieses Scheines muß diesen Ausweis stets bei sich führen.

The holder of this card is duly registered as a resident of the town of Gernrode and is prohibited from leaving the place designated. Violation of this restriction will lead to immediate arrest. Registrant will at all times have this paper on his person

Kennk. A 34630
Legitimations Nummer / Identity Card Number

Unterschrift des Inhabers / Signature of Holder

Right Index Finger

Daniel Van Dusen Maj.
Name and Rank / Mit Gov Officer, U.S. Army

16. Mai 1945
Datum der Ausstellung / Date of Issue

(Dies ist kein Personal-Ausweis und erlaubt keine Vorrechte.)
(This is not an identity document and allows no privileges.)

Residence permit when "caught" by the US Army in the Harz Mountains life in the Soviet zone would involve a wholesale deportation of the German engineers, their families, and everything relevant to jet engine development to Russia in October 1946. The destination was a town on the Volga southwest of Moscow that has since changed names a couple of times (today it is Samara) and was a secure, closed facility (an OKB) where the Germans had very limited freedom of movement. At the time, the Junkers engineers were working on a turbojet engine project labeled TL-012 which had, in fact, been the plan under the Reich Air Ministry during the war. Subsequently, the Russian development focused on the more powerful BMW 018, with very limited and primitive industrial resources, according to reports. There is mention in the correspondence of one person whose wife was not included in the roundup because she happened to be elsewhere and was consequently left behind. Instead, there was another woman who did go in her place—or so it was implied!

The kidnapped German engineers were held in Russia until around 1950, when their usefulness was exhausted and they were repatriated to the DDR. The last of the engineers returned in 1953. There, two of the leading engineers were noted to have landed in prison, presumably for having attempted to go to the West. The Iron Curtain was sewn shut tightly. The Russo-German jet engine development effort ultimately ended up being taken over by the Russian Kuznetsov engine company. This concern later built the powerful NK-12 turboprop engines for the Tupolev Tu-95 *Bear* bomber in that country's strategic arsenal, as well as other engines.

As far as the Germans who returned to East Germany, there was a keen desire to reestablish their prowess for building engines and airplanes. Such an effort was initiated toward a commercial airliner named the Baade 152 using the personnel resources who stayed, consisting mainly of Junkers aircraft people. The company, VEB Flugzeugwerke-Dresden, was started in 1955. The name VEB stands for *Volkseigenschaftbetrieb* (or "people-owned concern"; i.e., a state-owned company). The Baade 152 first flew in 1958. The design featured similarities to the Boeing B-47, with twin podded engines under each high wing. The airplane also used a bicycle landing arrangement with outriggers for stability. Curiously, the nose of the airplane featured a set of windows that might have allowed the airplane to serve as a bomber. It was, after all, the height of the Cold War. One prototype crashed in March 1959, while being viewed by government officials who were meant to be impressed. That crash as well as Russian desires to dominate a future commercial jet industry in their sphere led to the cancellation of the program.

Back to 1945 and our story, where Sig's future was foggy at best. The future of those who stayed in the East, as described above, was certainly not foreseeable, but some could have imagined it.

By this time, it must have become general knowledge to the Germans in our story that Germany was going to be occupied by the Allies in four occupation zones administered by the Americans, the Russians, the British, and the French. The boundaries of these zones were not of great concern, except for those around the Soviet Occupation Zone, where all this discussion was taking place. As US troops had conquered the local region and were to give it over to the Soviets, the question was whether to go west with the departing Americans or stay. Another important dimension of the times was also that Germany's eastern boundary was going to be redrawn. That, however, was not an issue for the Junkers engineers because it lay further east, a region that was not likely to be attractive as a place to continue life.

The discussions with the Allied representatives were intense but cordial. The American officer involved insisted that Sig understand that if he were to take advantage of the American offer to be transported west as the US vacated that part of Germany and turned it over to the Russians,

The ill-fated Baade 152 airliner. *Image from the Vintage Wings of Canada website*

he was doing it of his own free will and was free to change his mind. On briefing Mutti about the meetings, she stated bluntly, "Hier bleiben kommt nicht in Frage!" ("Staying here is out of the question!").

Sig did not object or respond immediately, but her viewpoint settled the matter. She wanted to be as far as possible from places where the Russians held sway. In the end, since both of my parents hailed from Darmstadt in the American Occupation Zone, with family members residing there, the decision made itself. Besides, a decision had to be made so that Sig could work and support his family. Employment at Junkers became irrelevant when the war ended. There was no work available as yet. The Russian plan to restart Junkers was just a promise at this point.

The summer of 1945 was also an interesting time for Germans in that the Allies had to figure out who was a criminal and who could participate in the formation of a new civil government free of a Nazi criminal history. The process was called denazification and involved a long questionnaire that struck the respondents as silly or absurd but, for the Allies, got people sorted out. The goal was to get the Allies out of the day-to-day management of civil affairs as quickly as possible. Civil administration was not something that the army felt very comfortable doing. Further, it would be smoother to have Germans familiar with customs and language do the work.

The process of identifying people who needed to be punished for criminal behavior must have been taxing for Allied authorities. Surely the conscripted German soldier was just a soldier. On the other hand, an Allied soldier seeing the lifeless body of a German soldier can be forgiven for thinking that there lies a dead Nazi. The reality was that most ordinary people just led ordinary lives without any control over the external parameters imposed by the Nazi hierarchy. Germans were not necessarily Nazis and Nazis were not necessarily only Germans.

The real Nazi criminals sometimes took care to successfully cover their tracks or simply escape to distant parts of the world, largely South America where dictatorial governments gave them refuge. Fortunately, many true Nazis faced trials or simply on-the-spot justice from those they injured. The terror organization that was the Third Reich was riddled with fanatic enforcement means where, even in the military, political officers ensured "proper" behavior by military leaders. Under such circumstances, it was risky to conclude that surrendering to the Allies is a better move than dying. During the war, it was hard and sometimes deadly to stay clear of government action enforcement but that was just what the imperfect process of denazification was intended to clarify. For ordinary civilians, it worked to move the country forward.

Apparently, the German engineers involved in jet engines came out clean and would be allowed to pursue matters as they saw fit. There was still the matter of functioning employers able to hire these unemployed technical people. Networking by mail was the order of the day, as a modicum of postal service was reestablished. Private telephones were still a rarity and service largely nonfunctional. Much correspondence in Sig's files deals with potential opportunities, some of them very nebulous.

It turns out that Dr. Anselm Franz, the leader of the Jumo 004 jet engine team, was in Dessau when the Americans arrived. He was quickly dispatched (Spring 1945) to the US under the auspices of "Operation Paperclip." He was accompanied by others, notably Dr. Heinrich Adenstedt, a metallurgist involved in the Jumo 004 engine, where his skills were surely employed in the design of the turbine. These two individuals will play important roles in Sig's travels to the United States a few years later.

Operation Paperclip involved the identification of about 1,600 technical people whose fields of expertise were of interest to the United States. The primary American motivation was to learn as much about technology that might be usefully employed in the still ongoing war in the Pacific. The list of fields covered was broad and included rocket engineers from the V-2 program in Peenemünde. While "Paperclip" is often associated with the transfer of Werner von Braun to the United States, that dimension is indeed a narrow aspect of its totality; many others were involved. Von Braun naturally earned disproportionate acclaim for his later role in the development of the Apollo Program that landed Americans on the moon. Initially, von Braun spent the years after the war at the US Army Redstone Arsenal in Huntsville, Alabama, where the emphasis was on military rocket development.

For those engineers who accepted the American proposal, preparations were made to go west. The plan was to be picked up at a date and time to be specified, and the family was to be ready to go. Each family was allowed 300 pounds of personal belongings. Others in the groups going west were airlifted into western occupation zones, ultimately destined to meet at Bad Kissingen, 200 miles to the southwest, the final location.

Sig was, by nature, a very conservative man. He was careful with money and always saved what he could. His young adulthood and the financial difficulties associated with growing up without a providing father molded him. By war's end, he had saved a substantial sum, now stashed in a bank. In his negotiations with US personnel, he insisted that a condition of his going was obtaining his funds from the bank. That is the way Mutti put it in her writings. Really? Would he have stayed if the money could not be wrested out of the bank? He tried a number of times to make the withdrawal but was refused because the banks were closed, even though there were staff on hand and the doors were, at times, open.

"I would like to make a withdrawal from my savings account," he requested.

"The bank is closed."

"When will it open?"

"Not today," was the curt reply.

The times were simply too turbulent for ordinary commerce to be possible. Sig explained his frustration to the US officer managing the transport. They went to the bank together, where the officials again refused. The officer reached down and laid his side arm on the counter without saying a word. The bank official got up, fetched the necessary forms, and waited while Sig filled them out. He then disappeared with them into the hinterlands of the bank and returned with a bundle of bills. The deal was successfully consummated.

It should be said that the funds in question were in Reichsmark, or RM for short. That continued to be the currency in Germany after the war ended, but the money was practically worthless. American cigarettes and food items were the real currency. These physical items were not the basis of a sound economy, so steps would be taken in 1948 to implement currency reform with the creation of the Deutsche Mark, or DM for short. Conversion would be allowed at a paltry exchange rate, disappointing nearly everyone who held RMs.

Jumping again ahead in history, it is this currency reform that finally ended the Western Allied relationship with the Soviet Union and stepped up the heat of the Cold War. The Russians wanted no part of creating a strong new German currency. They wanted the Germans to be dependent on their occupiers. Tensions subsequently led to the blockade of Berlin and the Berlin Airlift (June 24, 1948, to May 12, 1949). The blockade was a Soviet closing of all roads and railroads so that the population of Berlin would have to accept Soviet control or starve. Berlin was a "walled" city, with virtually no means to feed itself. It was the United States' determination to keep the western parts of Berlin in their domain and thereby keep the population of Berlin in the "West" that resolved the heretofore tense relationship between occupied Germany and the occupying West. That relationship had been difficult initially when neither side was very comfortable in it. The US military did not wish to be or pay to be an occupier. On the other hand, occupation was the reality for the Germans burdened with the hard-to-forget wartime hurt and misery. After the Berlin Airlift, involving the wonderful story of the "candy bombers," the relationship improved and grew very strong in the context of the new Cold War. America had placed its bet with Germans, at least those residing in the western occupation zones. At the time, Berliners were very grateful for the Western Allied intervention by air that the Russians could not block. Appreciation for the supply of food and fuel until the Soviets backed down was expressed clearly when President John F. Kennedy visited the city in 1963 and said, "Ich bin ein Berliner!" The sentiment was echoed by President Ronald Reagan, who stated emphatically, "Mr. Gorbachev, take down this wall!," when he visited Berlin in 1987. The wall was the infamous Berlin Wall constructed in 1961 to separate Berliners from Berliners, to separate Germans from Berlin, and most importantly, to keep Germans living in the Soviet Zone from escaping to the West. It was the tense focus of the Cold War adversaries for some time, until both sides agreed to just live with it. The world can thank Mikhail Gorbachev for acceding to the demand by Mr. Reagan, and later by the East German citizenry, without military intervention and certain bloodshed. My parents, sadly, did not live to see the fall of the wall in November 1989.

CHAPTER 14

Fateful Day

The day came: June 21, 1945. The handover to Soviet forces was to take place on July 1. A number of deuce-and-a-half-ton Dodge trucks showed up in Dessau, and our family, as part of the contingent of people going west, were loaded. It was the morning of a beautiful, warm day. The canvas cover had been removed from the rear of the truck so that travel would be relatively pleasant, with an open top. Two other families joined us in the truck, for a total of six adults, four children, and the permitted gear. This trip marked the first time I ever met an African American person—a soldier who also gave me my first orange and, if my memory serves well, my first Hershey bar.

The destination was to be Oberursel and then Bad Kissingen, where arrangements had been made to assemble the displaced engineers. Bad Kissingen is in Bavaria (fairly near Frankfurt/Main) and lies about 200 miles to the southwest of Dessau. Travel papers to that effect were issued to Sig for the entire family. It is not clear what the arrangements for work or future travel were going to be, but we were off. We sat on two rows of benches along the sides of the truck, facing inward, with a large heap of possessions in the middle. There were numerous suitcases, ammunition boxes converted into suitcases, and even somebody's treasured (child's?) mattress.

On the trip, the driver-soldier of our truck encountered a young woman who, during a stop, pleaded with him to allow her to hitch a ride to the west. Refugees and would-be refugees were everywhere, looking for rides to the west. She tempted him with a bottle (Mutti says it was whiskey; how would she have known?), and that settled the deal. The

The hotel in Bad Kissingen where the Allies assembled the German engineers in a modern photograph. The hotel has since been replaced by a bank. *Courtesy K. Eggers*

young woman got into the cab, and the driver proceeded to drain the bottle. The inevitable consequence of driving drunk eventually led to the driver's loss of control of the truck on a curve of the road. The truck went down an embankment and up toward the edge of a newly plowed field. The truck tipped over rather violently, and we were hurled out into the grassy landscape. I landed face first in the adjacent newly plowed field with a soil-caked eye and ended up with what turned out later to have been a concussion. As the mayhem settled down, my parents searched for my brother but could not find him. They panicked, and Mutti took her anger out on the deliriously drunk and nearly comatose driver by shaking him and yelling at him without effect. Much to Sig's credit, he did not lose his temper, even given his short fuse. Shortly after the initial mayhem, other trucks and jeeps in the convoy arrived at the scene. One of the newly arrived trucks was used to right ours with an assortment of chains and ropes, and under the frame, we found the unconscious body of my brother. He was put on the mattress we had in our truck and then loaded into a jeep together with my mother. She could barely hang on for the trip to a nearby hospital. A few miles away was the small town of Sömmerda, with a functioning medical facility.

Uli got x-rayed and it turned out he had a triple skull fracture, along with a broken collar bone. He obviously had to stay in medical care. The rest of the family was examined and released. My concussion was made obvious by my being served a bowl of fresh cherries by the hospital staff and my promptly returning those cherries into a toilet bowl: one of my earliest memories!

The decision was made between the military officers and my father that the safest approach was for him and me to proceed west with the military to avoid a tangle with the Soviets. Sig was issued travel papers the next day by the headquarters of the 34th Tank Battalion, US Army, stating that

> the bearer of this note, Siegfried Decher, was on his way to Oberursel, near Frankfurt to work on jet propulsion equipment for US Intelligence when the American truck in which he was being transported was wrecked. He should be sent on to Oberursel as soon as possible.

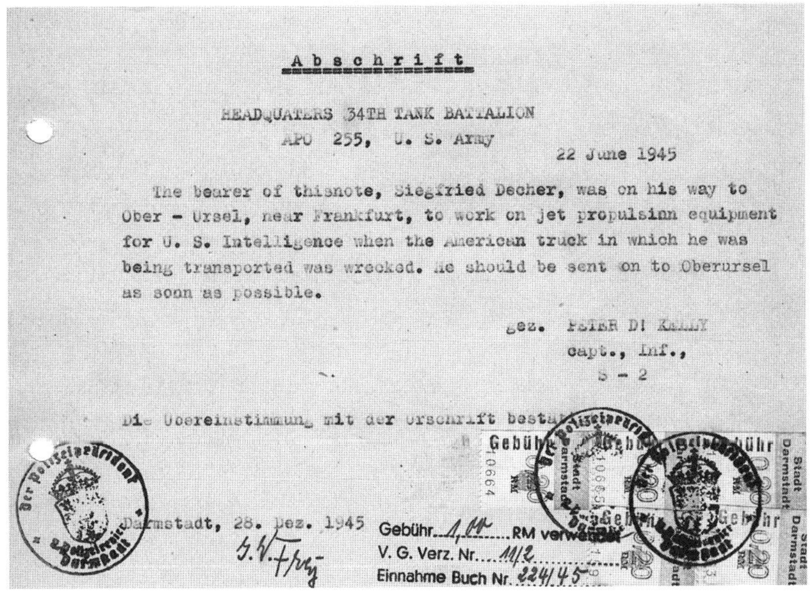

Abschrift

HEADQUATERS 34TH TANK BATTALION
APO 255, U. S. Army

22 June 1945

The bearer of thisnote, Siegfried Decher, was on his way to Ober - Ursel, near Frankfurt, to work on jet propulsinn equipment for U. S. Intelligence when the American truck in which he was being transported was wrecked. He should be sent on to Oberursel as soon as possible.

gez. PETER D! KALLY
capt., Inf.,
S - 2

Die Uebereinstimmung mit der Urschrift bestä[tigt]

Darmstadt, 28. Dez. 1945

Gebühr 1,00 RM verwendet
V. G. Verz. Nr. 11/2
Einnahme Buch Nr. 224/45

Travel papers after the accident, initiated by the US Army and made official by German civil authorities

An infantry captain signed the note, which was also adorned with a number of stamps and stamp imprints from German officials. With these papers, we resumed our trip out of the Soviet Occupation Zone.

Sig and I arrived in Darmstadt on June 26, and Sig was registered by the Military Government of Germany as a resident of the city. What overnight accommodations were employed for this five-day trip is forgotten, but I suspect that the military provided what was needed. It should hardly be surprising that Oberursel was a destination of interest for these aviation propulsion engineers. A factory there played a significant role in the development and construction of rotary piston engines used in World War I, which were appropriately named Oberursel engines. The engine manufacturing facility had focused on newer aircraft engines during the war.

Mutti stayed with Uli. After consulting with the Americans, the hospital staff recognized the need to keep the Russians from suspecting that the new arrivals were connected with a jet engine engineer headed to the American zone. They provided Mutti with a nurse's uniform to make her look like a member of the staff. The ruse was not entirely inappropriate because of Mutti's years of training and working as a nurse before she met Sig.

Uli remained unconscious for two days, and upon waking up, he recognized his mother and smiled. She engaged him in conversation about "Struwelpeter" nursery rhymes she knew he had learned, but would he remember them now? A recital of these rhymes by Uli caused Mutti to break into tears of happiness: he did not seem to have suffered brain damage.

The injury to his head caused drainage to issue from his left ear, so he had to stay prone with that ear down. The care regimen in Sömmerda went on for about a week. It was not yet July 1—when the handover was to happen. In the town was a regimental headquarters for the US Army, located in a city building. The military officials there were aware of my folks at the hospital and the American connection to them, but in spite of daily inquiries and requests by Mutti, she could not get transportation to Bad Kissingen to rejoin the family: no orders! Then, one morning, she went to the hospital, passing by the Army HQ. To her horror, the American flag was no longer flying and the building was empty. There went any hope of rejoining her husband and her other child. She returned to the hospital, making detours to see if traces of the US Army were to be seen, but alas, she had no luck. After an hour at the hospital, a doctor found her and informed her that there were two American soldiers looking for her with a stretcher and an ambulance standing by! Oh joy! They embarked as quickly as handling of the patient allowed and left town westward. On the way out, Mutti reports having seen drunken Russian soldiers in the streets. They had left just in time!

The reunion in Bad Kissingen was joyful. Uli was transferred to hospital facilities under American control, where he received very good care. He stayed prone on his left side for a few more days as he healed. While he was in Bad Kissingen, it was possible to have him lie near a window, outside which was an ever-changing parade of American military vehicles. I am told that I described for Uli the nature of these vehicles as they passed by or were parked within view. I apparently knew something about the US Army's vehicles. After four weeks or so, Uli was taken out in a stroller to a nearby park on a daily basis and was steadily improving.

In early September, the time finally arrived when Uli could go home, but the problem was that the family had no home. Where the family was quartered during Uli's recovery is unknown, but it surely was temporary. We were actually homeless, as were millions of refugees. People with intact dwelling units were strongly urged by the newly minted city governments to share as much as practical. And people did, for the most part. The best possibility for longer-term shelter was to move to Darmstadt and in with Sig's mother, his sister, and her two sons. They occupied their long-held apartment, where I was also stationed during part of the initial turmoil associated with the accident. It was tight but doable. The problem was finding food. There were children's ration allowances, which helped. The US authorities were also helping via the distribution of powdered milk and other necessities, though not in great quantities. Every little bit helped. All this time, Uli was recovering and relearning motor skills such as walking. His recovery was reasonably fast and complete.

As a family of four, in a house of eight, we stayed in Darmstadt until January 1946. Sig was contacted by people who wanted him to return to Dessau. The letters were glowing with promises of good living conditions and interesting work. These letters betrayed having been written by political officials and edited by censors. Sig saw what was written between the lines and declined.

There was also a disappointing postcard from the APWIU (the Air Prisoner of War Interrogation Unit, US Armed Forces in Europe), dated October 18, 1945. It stated:

> To Siegfried Decher, 1. In response to various inquiries received by us, we hereby inform you that there is no possibility at present of using your services. 2. We thank you for your cooperation.
> —Signed by a First Lieutenant, US Army

This was not the news Sig was hoping for. He had hoped that he could join Franz in the United States and continue to work with him on jet engines. The underlying reason for this postcard was that the war in the Pacific was over and the need or interest for German technical people to come to the United States had subsided substantially. The accident and the delay associated with caring for my brother served to cancel the trip to the United States with Franz and the others. In hindsight, it is hard to imagine how our lives would have differed, had we landed in America in 1945 rather than stayed in Europe.

A break in the search for employment finally came when a number of his colleagues shared news that the French government was looking to start something that would eventually result in the creation of a jet engine industry in France. There had been none before the war, but France was an early participant in the rich history of aviation more generally and felt the need to continue that tradition. Their competitive nature required active participation in the development of new jet engines. The role of the new engines in the design and capabilities of military aircraft was well appreciated. To that end, the French government had contacted Dr. Hermann Oestrich, who headed the unfinished development for the BMW 003 engine.

The connections with the US Army ended with a considerable amount of file correspondence having to do with "forced" (a better word might be "involuntary") evacuation from Dessau, for which the US Army had made arrangements for some financial reparations to the individuals involved. The funds were meant to compensate for household goods left behind when the people were transferred from Dessau to the West. Also considered were damages as a result of the US Army's handling of the evacuation. That aspect involved a series of costs associated with the accident. Sig obtained a fraction of the monies he requested. In retrospect, just getting the opportunity not to live behind the Iron Curtain would seem to have been sufficient compensation. Even for the time, the word "forced" or "involuntary" in its use to characterize the evacuation seems odd. At the time, the US Army insisted that Sig decide freely whether to go west with them; thus it might be argued that the trip west was voluntary and therefore would involve a reduced responsibility of the US Army. We may never know the details.

Assembly in Lindau

The French government moved ahead with plans to assemble a group of German aeronautical engineers. The descriptive title for the assembled people was Group "O" ("O" for Oestrich). The process involved two aspects: identification of the people to be involved and a location in France. The people were quickly identified, and Sig was among them. The others came primarily from BMW and from related German aircraft business enterprises that are now no longer functioning. The total number was about 150. While the French were looking for a good location, the engineers were moved to a suburb of Lindau on Lake Constance in Germany in order to start work. Lindau was located in the French Occupation Zone, where the French, as administrators, could make things happen. The move occurred in January 1946.

Housing was pulled together, and our family ended up in a multifamily house on the German-Austrian border. Its owners were involuntarily removed by French authorities on the premise that they were formerly Nazis. This gives some idea about the level of roughness involved in moving this project forward. Our assigned residence was the last house on the road to the toll gate into Austria. Food was still a problem, and Mutti tells of trying to negotiate for food with others in similar situations, but it was pretty futile: there was none to be had. Food and heat were still in very short supply six months after the cessation of hostilities. That spring, Mutti converted part of the yard into a garden whose soil she supplanted with dippings from the septic tank. At least vegetables would provide something to eat in the later months of spring and summer.

Mutti's pride was boosted with a harvest of the biggest and best vegetables that summer—thanks to access to the septic tank!

I recall playing with the other children and wandering in the nearby woods, unknowingly crossing the border and back again. The forest was a treasure trove of detritus from the war. There were discarded uniforms, presumably shed by soldiers escaping the conscription in the Wehrmacht during those last days. There were also weapons of various kinds; side arms, rifles, grenades, and other hardware. This was all very interesting to us as young boys, until Sig and the other fathers found out about our exploits. The woods became off-limits for playing. Fortunately, there were no mishaps.

This was also the time when I started first grade, with little in the way of memories except once getting a turn at the one set of colored pencils for the class, learning the colors and the numbers. To this day I associate those basic elements of learning with the color blue always evoking the number "4," among others.

The work location for the engineers beginning their work was in the nearby town of Rickenbach. The facilities were the former site of the Dornier factory. The town lent its name to a series of jet engines that were designed and built by the Group "O" engineers in the years that followed. Thus the first engine was the ATAR 101. The acronym stands for ATélier Aeronautique (aeronautical workshop) de Rickenbach. It was an improved and higher thrust version of the BMW 003. There were a number of ATAR engines to follow this start.

The war-ending treaty among the Allies and imposed on Germany carried the stipulation that no work that had the potential for military use could be carried out on German soil. Thus the jet engine enterprise would have to be moved to France. These were the new rules formalized on August 2.

In France, a site for the start of the new enterprise had been identified, but it was not ready for work to start, nor were the residences ready for the families. Thus the men were to leave alone, with their families left behind. Sig had received a travel document dated March 22, 1946. In anticipation of the coming move. It was a certificate by the "Direction Technique et Industrielle de l'Air":

> Mr. Siegfried H. Decher, born 2.11.1912 in Darmstadt is commissioned by the French Authorities of the French Occupation Zone. The allied authorities are requested to aid Mr. Decher in the execution of his mission and to protect him as well as his family. It is especially pointed out to facilitate their displacements (by any means of communication) in any way, to protect their property and to grant them exemption of any other personal taking up and any sequestration of their dwelling.

This document, in three languages, presumably allowed for safe travel in the various Western Occupation Zones, where Allied military control was still tight. It was signed in Lindau-Rickenbach by a French colonel. The text quote is exactly as written here, complete with grammatical and spelling vagaries associated with a translation of a French document into English.

As if to close the book on the wartime period, Sig received a letter in May 1946 stating that his termination date with Junkers was May 31, 1945. Some things took a while, or perhaps the people who remained in Dessau finally concluded that Sig was not coming back.

CHAPTER 16

On to France

The government had identified a set of buildings that were once a military barracks in central France on the Loire River as a suitable location. In French and German, the word *caserne* is used for such a military residence compound (barracks), and I will use that word here because it is short and to the point. The small town was Decize in the Départment of Nièvre. It appears that Julius Caesar was there and settled a dispute with the Decetiae, from whom the town retains its name. The town of a few thousand inhabitants is located about 180 miles south of Paris in a very rural setting.

The location of the caserne was on a hill overlooking the surrounding landscape near the former boundary (the Loire river in that area) between occupied France and Vichy France. Both of these political entities were controlled by the occupying Nazis until France was liberated in the summer of 1944. The wartime experience of the people was not good at the hands of the German occupation forces, who had resided at the caserne prior to the tide of war turning against them when the Wehrmacht called these troops to fight elsewhere. It is quite likely that the company was formed there, rather than started near Paris, because anti-German feelings were, at that time, still white-hot following the recent liberation of the city. Later, in the mid-1950s, the wartime suffering had begun to slide into the past and the company would indeed be moved to the Paris environs. For now (1946), the group was moved into a small-town environment where peaceful transition was more likely to be possible.

We were Germans living on what was once the boundary of two Frances, one directly conquered and the other governed by French men

The town of Decize from the air. The caserne is at the top, in the center. The Loire, on the bottom, flows to the left.

who acquiesced to Hitler and kneeled in submission. I was a child then, but adulthood allows reflection because reading about that time helps clarify matters, even though they can never be fully understood or reconciled. If I may be allowed a philosophical side trip, I want to briefly explore the reality of German Nazism had on Germans living in France after the war and even later in the United States.

A central question persists: What right has any man to steal from or kill another, when the latter just wants to live in peace, right where he is? Here, formal religious doctrine spells out the answer, but religious administration in the form of the church

Arrival of the men at the Decize train station. *Courtesy K. Eggers*

and similar institutions often fails, as it did in World War II, because its hold on power was in play. There are always those for whom the moral argument is moot and might is right.

During the Nazi era in Germany, there is abundant evidence that people in many countries, conquered or not, held positions that were either looking favorably at fascism or against it. In the United States, there were sympathizers for the Nazi cause. Henry Ford and Charles Lindbergh come to my mind, and they were by no means alone. Britain had its own set of people ready to step into government when all was lost after the Battle of Britain roared in English skies and Londoners suffered the pointless bombing by airplanes and crude missiles. Conversely, in Germany, there was a vigorous and determined opposition to Hitler. For far too many Germans, it was a futile and deadly effort.

France was conquered in 1940 by superior forces, as were countless civilizations before them. Armies that were strong and measured their prowess by the acreage of their domination were easily assembled by men of boundless egotism and minimal moral restraint. The presence of a conqueror will necessarily demand that the conquered decide to either accept and perhaps reinforce the conquest, or to resist it with the hope that a return to a situation resembling the past will be forthcoming in the future. That decision will pit one conquered citizen against another with the opposing view. That conflict is not merely an intellectual difference of opinion, but the foundation of a fight that was then, in many cases, deadly.

The events of 1944, when Paris was liberated, played out with violence when collaborators were hunted, shamed, punished, and sometimes summarily executed. Those French citizens bet on the wrong horse, but how were they to know that the Allies would eventually be victorious? The German power must have appeared to be invincible at one time, depending on what information one chose to believe. The course of war resolves all such conflicts, provided there are people willing to step up to right a wrong. The winners win and the losers lose. War is sometimes necessary to correct a wrong imposed on others for power, greed, and worse. The United States' decisions to enter both World Wars I and II were, in the mind of this German-American, morally correct decisions.

A larger question is brought into focus by peace: What next? Obviously, the moral right step is to punish criminals, but then, what is a criminal?

And by what laws? Those that were in effect at the time or those of the new present? A person might have betrayed another or helped in a material way to advance the cause of those in power to obtain food, or soap, or shelter. Is that a crime? Executing someone without due process will always be murder. Can betrayal ever be proven to the same standard as murder? The result is often the same.

My experience of witnessing the times after World War II is that people worked hard to forget by not talking about the past. Often this is a coping mechanism for those who might have done more for a just cause. An individual can never erase memory, but he can avoid reliving the past by not discussing it. What is done is done. No one can bring back the dead. Institutional memory is quite another thing. That memory must be preserved and allowed to be appreciated by the people who choose to learn about history. The people who suffered, who deal with guilt, or who want to forget what they witnessed may not want to visit the installations of institutional memory. Their children will. They will want answers to questions like: What was it like? What did you do? Where is or was my father? How did he die? And a thousand more. Most are unanswerable.

Personally, I am very proud of the present-day German instinct and practice not to forget what that country unleashed with the installation of memorial sites and protecting the right to speak truths. Importantly, Germans tend to teach their children about the sordid history of the past persecution of Jews, foreigners, the weak and infirm, and those with different cultural traditions. The aftermath of war is hopefully peace, a peace with a realization that war is a collective failure. The failure does not necessarily rest on all individuals overrun by the wave of war. Some surely, but mostly not, for the foremost motivation is survival, with moral standards intact, if possible.

It is this aspect of living in France after World War II as a German that dominates my thinking about the experience. A French merchant in his shop can come to the conclusion that the German customer standing in front of him is just a human being. He probably had nothing to do with the horror experienced or described in the newspapers, or with the suffering brought to his community by the invading army and the inter-French violence it unleashed. The customer was likely more human than German. Starting that minute, he has to get on with life as it is, not as he might have hoped it would be. Thus both have a reason to put knowledge and memory aside and begin a process that might end with forgiveness.

Looking at a vanquished Germany in 1945 is a little like being in a mythical china shop with a lot of breakage. The Allied armies restored quiet and thereby owned the breakage all around. As I write this, I am an American. As such, I proudly accept, ex post facto surely, some of the responsibility for the consequences of the war brought by the Allies. Americans did the right thing with the restoration of civility, justice in the form of Nuremberg and other trials, and finally economic stability with the implementation of the Marshall Plan. It helped that reality for Americans included staring at the Russian bear with designs on all of Europe. Sadly, American invasions thereafter did not always leave the affected countries in as positive a state of affairs. Vietnam and Iraq come to mind.

In this setting, the fathers got things ready for the subsequent arrival of their families. They arrived by train—an entire train used for the transport of people and furnishings. Additional trains brought more. The main train station was located a couple of kilometers from the destination, but fortunately, it was also served by a narrow-gauge railroad

The narrow-gauge railroad moving the engineers' belongings to the caserne. *Courtesy K. Eggers*

track running along the main road to a brick factory on the far side of town. A charming little steam locomotive, normally used for hauling clay tiles, bricks, and the like, came in handy for the last leg of the move to the front entrance of the caserne.

The men were first housed in a large garage that served as sleeping quarters. Food was provided, and then it was time to start work. Making the best of things, the men got the industrial aspects organized: the shop here, drafting room there, conference room over there, and so forth. The cleaning of the living quarters required attention, in part because of a serious and much-maligned infestation of cockroaches that was the subject of much humor for all the years to follow. There was time to organize politically for appropriate social order—committees to do this and that—and finally party time with plenty of French wine when the day was done. No women yet, though!

The rest of the family stayed in Lindau on the Austrian border for a time still characterized by hunger. Our diet was mainly potatoes and, later in the summer, fallen apples where no one had bothered to pick them up from the ground. I am quoted by Mutti as saying (in German, of course): "I don't want any potatoes, but my tummy does!" For a time,

A garage serving as a dormitory for the men. *Courtesy K. Eggers*

now past, I detested pan-fried potatoes as I grew older. To compensate for the absence of the fathers and husbands, the French government took a hand in making sure that food supplies for the families were of increased quality. Indeed, they gradually were, including a supply of wine for people who had not had a sip in years!

November 1946 finally came. The trip by the women and children to France was by train. Travel proceeded with interruptions of the relatively slow speed to even slower speeds. I would look out the window and notice that the train was crossing a river on a temporary bridge adjacent to a war-destroyed bridge. Some of them seemed to be in the process of being rebuilt. Others would have to wait. Was I excited about the move? A hard question since a child lives in the world as it is, and as long as parents nurture and protect, a child accepts the world on its terms. It was certainly hard for me to imagine what lay before me, a new language, new friends, new school...

The caserne was located about a mile outside Decize, an old Roman town that was situated on an island in the Loire, with an active river flow on one side and an overgrown floodplain on the other. The caserne, with its closely collocated working and living spaces, was an easy walk or bike ride into town. It was enclosed by a security fence, and there were provisions for a camp-like independence of operation within the compound. Included in the compound were two separate houses, for occupation by important personnel. Dr. Oestrich occupied one of these houses. While there were large entry gates leading to the residential area, they were never closed. In that area, there was a large woodshed supplied with fuel by the French government for the wood-fired stoves in the kitchen, the only source of heat. The men had to cut and split it. There was also a wooden building that was converted to a two-grade schoolhouse for the smaller children. It was the site of my first French schooling days, when I was still entirely ignorant of the French language and remember tearfully wondering how a life without communication skills could go on. A canteen, or better said a dispensary, sold ever-better and larger amounts of groceries as the years went by. Finally, there was a bathhouse where showers could be taken once a week separately by men and women. Initially, food was limited, but French red wine was available, as were continued rations of American powdered milk in their blue-green cardboard cans.

Map of France (circa 1941) showing locations of Decize and the inter-French boundary. The whole of France became occupied by the Nazis at the end of 1942. *Andreas Illert*

The French named the caserne complex "Cité Voisin," after the famous French aviator Charles Voisin and his airplane manufacturing company from a time before and during World War I. Our address was therefore Cité Voisin, Bât. (short for *building*) D, Decize, Nièvre. No postal code! Later (circa 1950), it became the home of the firm SNECMA, a French acronym for the National Society for the Study and Construction of Aviation Motors.

CHAPTER 17

Life in Decize

The caserne was a collection of six three-story buildings, each with three external entries: buildings A through F. Each entry gave access to six apartments facing the central area and looking out to the rear. Small balconies were part of the upper four of those six units. In all likelihood, an early task by the men when they arrived was to determine who was going to occupy which apartment. We ended up on the top floor, which seemed quite desirable for the view and the absence of footstep noises from above. The units were modest, ours having two bedrooms, a living room, and a family room and kitchen. A single wood-fired stove served for cooking and heating needs. There was no bathroom as such, just a toilet. Most daily bathing was done at the kitchen sink. There were no appliances, and the summer heat required adapting an old galvanized sheet steel-lined ammunition box to house a chunk of ice to preserve perishable food. It was a true ice box. In the first years, even that robust but primitive refrigeration method was not available, nor was it required, because butter was scarce. There was little else to put into it. Milk, for example, was purchased daily. Later when ice was available in town, I was typically tasked retrieve and carry chunks of ice on the back of my bike.

Just prior to the men moving in (there were also about seven professional women involved, as I recall), the caserne served for a short period as a POW camp. Some of the detainees were still present when the women and children arrived. These presumably former Wehrmacht troops were likely Germans or non-German conscripts who had, by then, not been repatriated, in part because they may not have had a place to return to. While they were there, barbed wire fencing surrounded their quarters,

An aerial view of the Cite Voisin complex from a postcard. The date is the late 1940s. To the upper right is the Loire valley. The woodshed is on the bottom, in the center. The former POW camp is at seven o'clock. The commissary is the building at nine o'clock, while school for the young children is barely visible at ten o'clock, between the two large housing units. The workplace is off the picture to the left. The rear of the building at four o'clock became a complex of gardens.

Firewood distribution for the coming winter. *Courtesy K. Eggers*

with openings through which inquisitive children made unauthorized, overlooked visits. The men served as manual laborers for a variety of functions. Some earned extra money from products they made in the wood and metal shops. We still have some in our possession: a cutting board, a handspun aluminum cooking pot, and an aluminum trunk. It appears that when the war ended, aluminum became a common material that was no longer needed for manufacturing airplanes. Outside the times they had to work to compensate for room and board, these POWs were relatively free to move about. They left relatively soon after the arrival of the families.

The parents describe the years in Decize after the war as their happiest. Peace reigned, the work was rewarding, there were lots of social companions for adults as well as for children. The photo albums depict parties with costumes on occasions like Fasching (Mardi Gras in France) and occasions to celebrate this or that, usually with homemade music made by the participants. Sig would often be called on to play his accordion. Socially, our world in the caserne was separate from that in the town. The central grass area between the buildings served for sports, nominally volleyball, and activities for the children sometimes organized by the adults. Some photos show Sig learning about the rules of volleyball and joining his son in an egg-carrying race.

The German prisoners of war. *Courtesy K. Eggers*

The food situation was improving every year, and money was being saved. Some of the furnishings arrived from our past dwelling places by means unknown. Eggers reports that the French made the retrieval of furniture into a military mission and recovered lost items from the Soviet zone by some means where the Russians could not object. Our apartment was again furnished with some of the items we had in Dessau.

For the children, the learning of a new language was quick, though not necessarily painless. Two French teachers were hired to deal with the youngest and teach the new language to the middle-aged kids. In that group, I remember the tears associated with not understanding anything, but those passed quickly. It did not take long until the children in this large community spoke French among themselves and German with their parents and other local adults. The two lovely women teachers, Mademoiselles Bérard and Montaron, found their way into the hearts of all the children and adults who encountered them.

The children were especially fortunate in that there were a lot of children in the various age groups, so that one never longed for playmates. In my age group, around 6–12 years, there were a number of kids who played with toy cars on roads scraped onto the sidewalk footing. Best of all was the freedom to explore the surrounding countryside, of which

The adults organize to play a game of volleyball. Sig is on the far left.
Courtesy K. Eggers

A multitude of children in summertime play. The author is in a black cap and suspenders, in front of Sig launching the runners. *Courtesy K. Eggers*

there was plenty. We ventured toward the Loire, through cattle pastures, exploring the twists and turns of the wild river. We also ventured into nearby forest lands, some of which were riddled on hillsides, with what looked like ditches to remind one of trench warfare. That might have been connected with the proximity of the boundary between occupied and Vichy France. Such wanderings were safe, and the parents had no reservations about seeing us disappear for whole afternoons at a time.

In the summer, the Loire was frequently visited for swimming on Sundays with the parents. On one such occasion, I recall father hanging our shirts on the cattle pasture fence only to find that one of the kids' shirts went missing. It was discovered half hanging out of a cow's mouth, the other half having disappeared into the dark insides of the ruminant. My father grabbed the visible part of the shirt and pulled, yielding a shirt with lots of holes, as if it had been a shotgun target!

Bicycles were the way to get around, especially for the children. I used my first bike (acquired around 1947) to travel to school and to town when more complete shopping was to be done at a bakery, two book and newspaper stores, and establishments for dry goods, ice, ice cream, and other needs. Bicycling was different then; no need for bike locks and no helmets! A helmet might have been useful when on one of my descents from the caserne into town I hit a curbstone and went over the handlebars at speed. It appears the damage was not permanent.

The initial period when the kids my age went into town to go to school at the Ecole Communale was difficult. We had to run the gauntlet of French kids hurling insults and rocks for being German as we proceeded. The time for that was mercifully short as the inevitable intimacy grew, and it was generally realized that there was little point in acrimony. In particular, the town merchants also realized that 150 German engineers made for customers with salary money from the government. Peace settled rather quickly, and before the years of the contracts for the engineers were out, there were a number of marriages across the two cultures.

Bicycle mobility fostered further social encounters with the local French children in the modest home of the local priest. Activities there were simply hanging out and often included trading cards that were included in the popular "Chocolat Menier" tablets we devoured. These cards were meant to be assembled into whole pages, each constituting *Fables de la Fontaine* (Aesop's fables for English speakers). I still have a chalk portrait of myself at that age, drawn by the priest. Trips to the two local movie theaters were always a great treat for kids who went there in groups and without parental oversight. American movies with voice-overs or subtitles were sometimes the fare, usually cowboy movies.

Unfortunately, when I finished fifth grade, I was not advanced to sixth due to poor grades and had to do fifth over again. I was, at the time, not great academically. The courses included algebra, physics, and chemistry, along with others. Among these was a mandatory foreign language which, in this school and time, was German. Considering the state of Franco-German relations after the war, that fact was interesting, and it served to expose me to written German. My retaking of math and science classes allowed me to do well in these subjects the second time around, and since I later retook them again in the United States, where they are offered later in the American curriculum, I did well there again.

The author during the Decize days, circa 1948

For the adults, I recall parents taking a ski vacation in the Massif Central of France, naturally without children. The skis Sig used were surplus German, white-painted, wooden ones, presumably intended for the Eastern front. As the 1940s ended, people started buying motorcycles and later cars. The cars were small, as typified by the Renault 4CV. Sig started with a small motorbike and a moped for Mutti. Their first summer adventure in 1950 was to tour southern France with Uli on the rear of the motorbike. There was no room for me in this parade, so I was dispatched to a summer camp on the Atlantic Ocean island of Oléron, where I, at least according to surviving pictures, memories, and saved postcard correspondence, was miserable in spite of beautiful water and beaches. At this camp, I distinctly recall that every breakfast consisted of a bowl of milk, hot chocolate, or coffee into which a big piece of a French baguette was dipped and subsequently eaten as cleanly as possible. The summer's highlight was an unpleasant and scary camp exchange visit with another camp that was thoroughly focused on hammer-and-sickle communism. It was also my first and only opportunity to watch the slaughter of a pig. On the pleasant side was the chance to dance in a tub of grapes to reduce them to juice. A 1950 Bordeaux (region), I believe!

The following year, Sig decided to buy a car large enough for all of us. The minimalist car he acquired in 1950 was a Citroën 2CV. Two cylinders provided all of 9 horsepower, with which it was hard for the car to exceed 40 mph, even downhill! It did allow for a summer trip to nearby sights and later to Spain and to Austria. Sig was a keen tourist and enjoyed photographing what there was to see in the world. Between trips, there were multiple occasions when the valves of the overworked engine had to be replaced or fixed. The car was primitive but, with care and maintenance, adequate. These cars can still be seen in France today and occasionally in the United States, where they never met various safety requirements but somehow got past US customs.

The trip to Spain in 1951 involved a memory I enjoy recalling. We were just about the only tourists to be found in the country. It was still a time to recover from the war that had devastated Europe. Hotels were a seldom-used option, and we consequently almost always camped in the car and a tent. On one particular evening, we found an agricultural side road where we decided to stay the night. There was no one to ask for permission. There were no buildings nearby, but we were noticed. During a camp stove dinner, a group of "natives" arrived along the road, and a nervous Sig thought that we were in for it. It turns out they were nearby farmers bringing water, bread, and wine to the visiting strangers! This was in Franco's Spain. We were unusual visitors, and they were curious and friendly.

Sometime during the period of currency reform in Germany, Sig's saved funds were finally converted from Reichsmarks to Deutschmarks—unfortunately, at a deep discount. In that time frame, he also submitted one of the more significant patents he had developed at Junkers and got the patent accepted by the French. The patent concerned the jet engine control mechanism described earlier. The US patent was later (1954) awarded to Sig and to Wolfgang Stein, who worked together at Junkers and SNECMA and would collaborate again later in the United States at AVCO-Lycoming. Stein's story thus parallels Sig's in professional ways, but not much more can be said about his path through life. While Stein's children and the Decher boys played together in France, we lost contact after emigration to the United States. Stein's name is nevertheless noteworthy, as we will note as the story proceeds.

In Decize, the technical work of the engineers was focused on the design of the ATAR 101 engine. The manufacturing facilities were in other parts of France because there was little in the way of facilities required in Decize. In the documentation of the time, Sig and Stein were prominently identified as two of the important designers of this engine. At the end of the design process came building and testing it. That was successfully accomplished in 1948.

As the time approached the end of the five-year employment contract with the French State, times were steadily improving, and they called for changes. Group "O" formally became SNECMA, a corporate undertaking that was to be weaned of direct financial support from the state. The first task was the need to manage the renewal of commitments to individual engineers—who was going to stay with the organization and who was not. It was clearer than it was in 1946 who was central to the work at hand; thus decisions had to be made. With economics improving in Germany, some engineers longed to return to their home country. On the French side, the political scene was also changing in that it was a time for greater participation by French engineers in this French undertaking. There was a small number of French involved from the beginning, but it was time to change the center of gravity of the personnel. Finally, the time was one of economic turbulence associated with labor unrest that lent pressure on jobs in national French politics. All this led to a reduction of the number of German engineers at SNECMA, and Sig was happy to learn that he was to be able to stay.

For Sig, the situation had an additional dimension involving his role in the senior technical management of the ongoing development efforts. It appears that Sig was hoping to play a larger role in whatever was going to be happening from a technical viewpoint, but Dr. Oestrich did not give him sufficiently warm indications that might lead his future in that direction. In short, he was looking for a promotion.

On the other hand, Sig never gave up on the idea of working with Dr. Franz. Additional responsibilities would surely have been secured, had he been able to join Franz in the United States. Instead, the connection with Franz at the end of the war was nebulous only because Franz went to the United States while Sig could not because of the accident. A formal relation existed between the two men, as Sig had been appointed as "representative in Germany" of Dr. Franz in technical matters, "should they arise." They didn't, but Sig felt the connection. The reality was that Sig really enjoyed working with Franz and hoped to work with him again. To that end, Sig, Dr. Heinrich Adenstedt, and Franz kept in contact throughout the time Sig was in France.

Sig's connection to Dr. Franz following the war's end was cited in his postwar correspondence with people seeking to get him to return to Dessau as a reason he could not rejoin the group remaining there. That was, however, simply a good excuse to stay clear of any situation that involved living in Soviet-occupied Germany.

Franz and Adenstedt were initially installed at Wright Field in Ohio, where they were debriefed on matters associated with the Jumo 004. When that process was complete, the two men (and possibly others) primarily did consulting work for American firms tackling the new challenges of building jet engines. At that time, these ex-Junkers engineers also focused on developing a contract with the US military for the production of a relatively small turboshaft engine aimed at use in helicopters. Helicopters were retained in the US Army as a part of military aviation that was not incorporated in the US Air Force when it was created in late 1947. Thus they worked to develop a proposal for the development of an engine with an output of about 600 horsepower for the US Army. Until a contract was actually issued, no commitment to Sig could be made.

In the meantime, Sig decided to leave SNECMA at the end of 1952. For him and our family, that decision meant parting ways with the colleagues and friends that had for so long been a part of life. A life history written by my friend Karsten Eggers, about his father Gerhard, noted that we lived at the same addresses in Dessau and in Gernrode, and very near each other in Decize. Gerhard Eggers was also active at Junkers. Times were changing, and old friends were going to be missed.

SNECMA, as a firm, went on to build a number of jet engines that paralleled the developments of the technology elsewhere, primarily in Britain and the United States. The ATAR engines SNECMA built were successfully incorporated in the designs of numerous, notably French, military jet aircraft. In the decade following Sig's departure, many of the German engineers, including Eggers, returned to Germany to an aviation industry that played its role in the Cold War. Some stayed in France and the firm became, within the NATO and commercial contexts, a thoroughly French undertaking. It went on to design and build large turbofan engines in a partnership with General Electric. The CFM-56 engine was widely used in commercial airliners and incorporated the high-bypass fan concept that Sig helped develop, as we shall see later in our story. Another major contribution to commercial aviation was SNECMA's role in building (in partnership with Bristol) the engines for the Concorde supersonic airliner. In time, the company name was changed to Safran, with an international reach.

To close out the topic of the Gruppe "O," we note that it included a number of the engineers who designed the various rocket engines that were tried, unsuccessfully one might add, to power German aircraft in the waning days of the war. The rockets worked, but the implementation was militarily faulty. These same people were the beginnings of the long and successful history of rocket propulsion for various commercial, scientific, and military purposes launched by the later European Space Agency and others.

Sig's decision to seek employment elsewhere wound its way into the grapevine. In Germany, times had also improved sufficiently in economic terms, since the currency reform was taking hold and the country was beginning its ascent to becoming a well-oiled economy. People were starting new companies, and they were looking for skilled people. A colleague from Junkers had contacted Sig about joining a concern building small reciprocating engines for a variety of markets. The offer was attractive, and Sig needed to make a decision. While working with reciprocating engines was not his favorite area, he decided in March 1952 to accept the offer from ILO Werke, based in Pinneberg just outside Hamburg.

Possible employment options included working in the United States. It was suggested by one of Sig's colleagues, who became a professor at the TH Darmstadt, that working at the Allison Division of General Motors in Detroit might prove to be a good move. This opportunity was not consummated in time to avoid moving to ILO in Germany, and thus another opportunity was lost to have moved to the United States.

Shortly thereafter, in July 1952, Adenstedt reported that a US Army contract was approved and that AVCO Corporation would form a gas turbine division to carry out the work. This effort was initially centered in the Lycoming engine plant in Williamsport, Pennsylvania. It was soon moved to Stratford, Connecticut, where an engine plant was already in operation, however at low capacity, making Curtiss-Wright R-1820 piston aircraft engines. The market for these engines was shrinking, and production ultimately ceased in 1958.

Franz and Adenstedt consulted with Sig on getting him to the United States, and a deal was made. The work was simply too good and interesting for Sig not to jump into. On August 18, 1952, the president of AVCO (S. B. Withington) wrote, stating that Adenstedt is authorized to negotiate a contract for one year (presumably renewable) for the development of "a gas turbine." The following is a direct quote:

> Briefly, the project is classified so we can't tell you about it. You will be working on basic research and "special components." Military clearance will be initiated upon your arrival. If you elect to accept employment, contact the US Embassy in Frankfurt.
>
> At the proper time, we will make application to the Attorney General of the United States for your entry into the United States under Sec. 204 of Public Law 414, the "Immigration and Nationality Act," which becomes effective December 24, 1952. Under Sec. 203

and 204 of this Act, immigrants with special skills that will be substantially beneficial to the welfare of the United States can be given preference on the quota list.

Unfortunately, Sig had signed a one-year employment contract with ILO, and they would not let him out of it. ILO felt they had a good man, and they wanted to keep him. They thought that Sig could grow to like the work and the people working with him and would stay. His employment contract was to start in December of 1952, coincident with his termination date at SNECMA. Sig brought the matter to his friend and school colleague, who had become a lawyer, to assist him with the situation. Sig was concerned about the consequences of breaking the contract and, in particular, about a future with restrictions on him due to secrecy or noncompete clauses. Sig offered to help ILO find a suitable replacement. The secrecy issue turned out not to be a concern if he fulfilled his employment contract for the year as required and, during this time, was shielded from work that might be sensitive for him to take elsewhere. AVCO even offered a monetary settlement to get Sig out of the contract, to no avail. Thus, in December 1952, he started at ILO and simultaneously handed in his notice of intent to terminate his employment in December 1953. AVCO, for its part, kept its offer open until February 1, 1954.

For me, the move to Germany sheds some light on Sig and his approach to parenting. At his urging, my brother and I were shipped off to a boys' home in Wertheim, Germany, so that we were not in the way of the turmoil of packing and moving. Apparently, that process involved almost three months, a time in which my favorite possession, my bicycle, was sold without my having a say. It was apparently too cumbersome, and it was decided that I might not need it!

The boys' home to which we were sent was religiously based (named after one of the Reformation's architects), fairly rigid, and difficult to adjust to. I suppose that it might have helped us to be more familiar with the (to me) newish German language, but I was lonely and the proximity of an aunt I saw just once provided no consolation. At Christmastime, the family was reunited.

Interlude in Germany

So it was that the family stayed in the town of Pinneberg for a year. My brother and I went to German schools, where the pedagogy was tougher and certainly difficult to adjust to. I was to be excused from Latin and from English courses in the eighth grade that I entered midway in the academic year. The class I was to join had studied these languages a whole year earlier. German language instruction was significantly more intense. After all, we were now in Germany! Academically, the year was hard, but as a benefit, I had to take a train, with steam locomotive propulsion, to nearby Elmshorn where the school was located, and that was certainly a happy dimension of going to school. I loved trains. Uli, being younger, attended a local school.

The nearby city of Hamburg still had hills of rubble from the war's bombing in the center strips of its wide roads and other places where there was room to dump debris. Nevertheless, it was a worthy destination for expeditions of various kinds. For Sig, the stay in Germany was marking time and getting ready for immigrating to the United States. There were visits to consulates for interviews, medical exams, paperwork, fingerprints, job application forms, and packing. In his files were copies of documents he had to submit to American authorities. These, dated May 1953, included a list of the names of organizations to which he belonged, especially those in the years the Nazis were in power:

Jugendnational Bund 27–33 [The numbers refer to years, 1927 etc.]. An organization akin to scouting.

Hitler Jugend (Hitler Youth) 33–35. The modified and strongly politicized scouting organization when the Nazis came to power.

DAF (Deutsche Arbeitsfront) 36–45 (no office). The German Labor Front was the National Socialist trade union organization that replaced the various trade unions of the Weimar Republic. Sig stated that it was required to belong to this organization in order to be employed by Junkers or any other industrial organization.

NSV (National Sozialitische Volkswohlfahrt) 36–45 (no office). This social welfare organization was created in the Third Reich. He was a paying member of the NSV.

German Society for Engineering (Verein Deutscher Ingenieure, or VDI). A professional engineering society focused on advancing knowledge and educating its members.

Lilienthal Society. The Lilienthalgesellschaft für Luftfahrtforschung (Lilienthal Society for Flight Research) was originally known by other names. Ludwig Prandtl, the famous German aerodynamicist, was involved in the founding of one of the earlier organizations, and the membership list is a "who's who" of the German air establishment, even in the days prior to the war. Membership applications were reviewed at the time by a committee, and it was indeed an honor to have been approved. The namesake, Otto Lililienthal, was one of aviation's pioneers, who contributed much to the understanding of flight through the use of gliders. Unfortunately, in 1896, he met his maker in a gliding accident from an isolated hill, attempting to launch himself in any direction dictated by the wind. He is credited by some with formulating the initial concepts of a rigid wing.

ASC (Academic Sports Club). Sig was a member of this club since his university days in Darmstadt. It fostered athletic and social events.

Sig certified that he was *not* a member of the NSDAP (The Nazi Party).

Our mother Else was noted to have been associated with the German Red Cross in the years 1926–36.

That formality must have been stressful to complete, for it had to be honest and complete. It was accepted as such, and we could move on and plan for the upcoming voyage to the United States. This time we were not shielded from the mayhem of packing! We, the children, were told not to mention the coming emigration to our friends, in order to keep things simple, whatever that might have meant. In preparation for the life to come, father presented us children with American money: dimes and quarters made of real silver! Privately, my brother and I had weekly tutoring in British English that hardly seems to have been effective in retrospect but was, I suppose, helpful. I can honestly say that I later learned more American English from the movies on board our ocean liner and, once we reached the shore, hanging out with American playmates watching television. Total immersion was always the best way to learn a new language, and television made the process painless.

Among my memories, I recall knowing where I was when Stalin died: on the Elmshorn station platform where the commuter train took me home after school. It seems that even to this thirteen-year-old it was a momentous event for reasons that surely sank in later. That memory takes its place among other rememberings of where I was when President Kennedy was assassinated, when the space shuttle *Challenger* was lost, and on September 11, 2001.

The ILO company ended up being very successful in manufacturing small air-cooled piston engines that were a good match for motorcycles and snowmobiles. The American firm Rockwell bought ILO (in 1959) because of its interest in manufacturing snowmobiles. Sig, later and in the United States, ran across a snow machine that had the cooling fan he designed. Later competition from Japanese engines ultimately led to the demise of the German ILO engines. ILO's fortunes sank further after Germans learned to love automobiles more than motorcycles. Its doors finally closed in 1990, and so it seems that Sig chose well not to stay with ILO in Germany. On a visit in 2016 to Pinneberg, weeds were silent witnesses on the factory site, and the house where we lived was gone.

During the Pinneberg time in Germany, Sig carried on a vigorous correspondence primarily with one of his colleagues from Junkers who had gone on to the United States with Franz. The subject concerned the conditions of life in the United States, what to bring, what not to bring, electricity voltage differences, furniture, camera gear, and more. Should we bring our dog? What about school for the boys? And so on and so forth. It seems that for him the prospects were exciting.

Our family's last days in Germany were challenging. Correspondence revealed a plea for assistance from US shores because by November the visa applied for in March still had not been issued. If travel was to be accomplished in January, the visa had better come soon! It finally did in time to sell the car, a very cheap (or should I say a "low, short-term investment") two-door Lloyd with plywood doors. This was more powerful than the 2 CV we had in France, with all of its 13 horsepower from a two-cylinder, two-stroke engine that gave the car a maximum speed of 47 mph!

The dominant activity was packing, getting rid of things that were not going, and finally, making arrangements for a friend and colleague to take us to Bremerhaven for the launch to the United States. The departure date was January 23, 1954, with planned arrival on the twenty-eighth in New York. Arrival was just ahead of the date of February 1, to which AVCO had agreed to hold Sig's position open. It is hard to believe that they would have backed out, had the deadline actually been missed.

It appears that January was not a busy travel season, and so it was that we secured first-class tickets for crossing the Atlantic on SS *United States,* the fastest ship plying the North Atlantic and the pride of the American passenger liner fleet.

A letter from Sig's mother (Oma) arrived just prior to our departure, expressing the pain of separating across the large Atlantic Ocean and

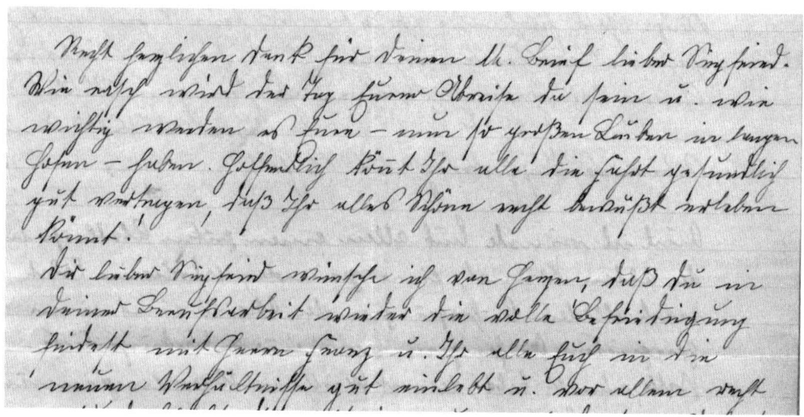

Recht herzlichen Dank für Deinen lb. Brief lieber Siegfried.

Letter to Sig written by his mother at the time of his departure for the United States. It begins: "Recht herzlichen Dank… " The letter is reproduced and translated in the text, with the author's comments in parentheses.

some important concerns about the traditional family religious faith. Years later, that concern turned to be variously valid for her grandchildren. Some chose to move away from faith altogether, some chose to actively pursue the ministry, and still others chose to join the Catholic Church, surely causing Oma's eyebrows to be raised from wherever she might be watching:

My dear children and grandchildren,

Hearty thanks for your loving letter, dear Siegfried. How quickly the day of departure will come and how important it will be for your boys, now in long pants! I hope you will go through the voyage with good health so that you can experience all that is beautiful.

For you, dear Siegfried, I wish with all my heart that you will again enjoy a very satisfying professional experience with Mr. Franz and that you adjust well to the new conditions and, above all, stay healthy. On this score, you surely have already collected considerable experience (in France)!

Pass on my greetings to uncle Emil (Oma's brother) and Margret Ott. We see on the map that you (will) live far from them (in Cleveland, Ohio). Hopefully you will soon find a good place to live. How nice that you can take Lumpi (our dachshund) with you so that he may remind you a tiny little bit of the homeland.

Please be so kind as to let us know by airmail of news of your safe arrival. I will be with you in thought and prayer and asking that we will meet again, while still healthy, at some undetermined, future time.

I do not want to be nagging before the departure, but your old mother pleads from the deepest part of my heart, that you stay true to the old faith (Protestant) of the parent house and that you will educate your children in it.

May God protect you and send his blessing with you. In spirit, I take you all in my arms and give you a hearty goodbye kiss.

Your mother, Oma
P.S. How many days will the ship take?

Our departure for the United States in January 1954 was momentous for our family members remaining in Germany. We were going to be missed, and it was unclear whether return visits were going to be possible in the foreseeable future. At that time, North America was, in practical terms, a long way from Europe. The ship was to take us crossing the Atlantic on her thirty-fifth voyage.

The crossing was rough and the subject of much family lore. My parents were pretty much done in by seasickness, but Uli and I, at least as far as I can recall, quickly accommodated to the rocking motion of this very large ship. We went to a lot of movies and learned a bit of English while watching films in technicolor. We even tried to go swimming one day, only to find out that the pool water obeyed the same laws of physics as the ship, splashing over the sides of the pool and hitting the walls as we entered the pool area. So much for that! The food was good and American: I had corn flakes with strawberries one morning—a first! We lost a day of travel time when we were fogged in prior to entering Long Island Sound, which made for good acclimatization to a steadier floor and allowed us to leave our sea legs somewhere in the Atlantic. We were a little worse for wear because January is rough on the North Atlantic, even in first class!

Sig was not alone in joining the Lycoming people in Stratford, Connecticut. It seems that Wolfgang Stein, the coinventor on the "onion" patent who had worked with Sig in France, was already part of the team. He and his family went to the United States in 1953. It is a bit of a mystery how Sig and Stein were not invited to the United States until the contract was in hand, because conversations must have taken place for the two men in Germany to help structure the proposal into something that the US Army would like.

Stein was an excellent engine configuration engineer who, in this case, capitalized on the basic ideas developed by Hans von Ohain in designing the engine that first flew in a jet airplane, the Heinkel He 178. He is credited with the unusual engine configuration of the Lycoming T53 turboshaft engine that was to arise from the new enterprise. That arrangement involved the use of a radial flow compressor in the last compression stages and a reverse flow combustor. These features made the engine compact and light in weight. They also allowed easy access to the hot section components for maintenance. The appeal of the radial

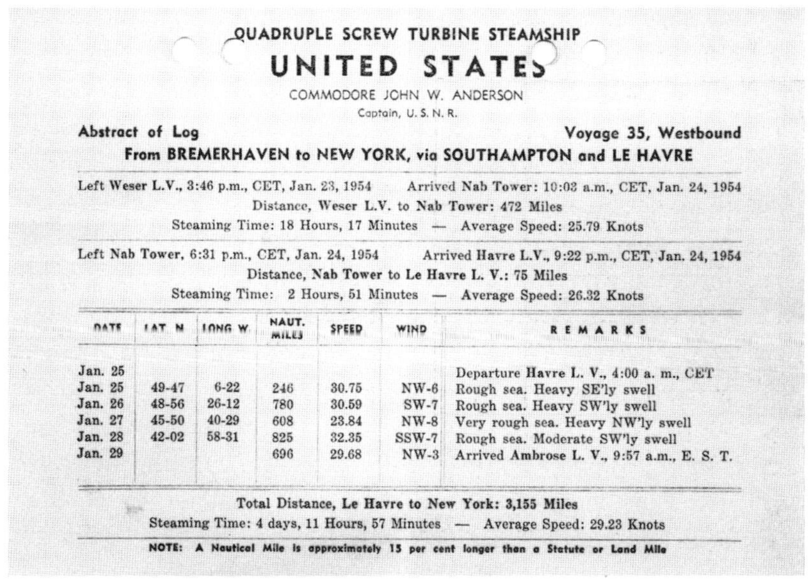

QUADRUPLE SCREW TURBINE STEAMSHIP

UNITED STATES

COMMODORE JOHN W. ANDERSON

Captain, U. S. N. R.

Abstract of Log — **Voyage 35, Westbound**

From BREMERHAVEN to NEW YORK, via SOUTHAMPTON and LE HAVRE

Left Weser L.V., 3:46 p.m., CET, Jan. 23, 1954 — Arrived Nab Tower: 10:03 a.m., CET, Jan. 24, 1954

Distance, Weser L.V. to Nab Tower: 472 Miles

Steaming Time: 18 Hours, 17 Minutes — Average Speed: 25.79 Knots

Left Nab Tower, 6:31 p.m., CET, Jan. 24, 1954 — Arrived Havre L.V., 9:22 p.m., CET, Jan. 24, 1954

Distance, Nab Tower to Le Havre L. V.: 75 Miles

Steaming Time: 2 Hours, 51 Minutes — Average Speed: 26.32 Knots

DATE	LAT. N	LONG. W	NAUT. MILES	SPEED	WIND	REMARKS
Jan. 25						Departure Havre L. V., 4:00 a. m., CET
Jan. 25	49-47	6-22	246	30.75	NW-6	Rough sea. Heavy SE'ly swell
Jan. 26	48-56	26-12	780	30.59	SW-7	Rough sea. Heavy SW'ly swell
Jan. 27	45-50	40-29	608	23.84	NW-8	Very rough sea. Heavy NW'ly swell
Jan. 28	42-02	58-31	825	32.35	SSW-7	Rough sea. Moderate SW'ly swell
Jan. 29			696	29.68	NW-3	Arrived Ambrose L. V., 9:57 a.m., E. S. T.

Total Distance, Le Havre to New York: 3,155 Miles

Steaming Time: 4 days, 11 Hours, 57 Minutes — Average Speed: 29.23 Knots

NOTE: A Nautical Mile is approximately 15 per cent longer than a Statute or Land Mile

The official Atlantic crossing trip card. Note the remarks.

flow compressor stage was attractive for the army that was likely going to be operating the engine in the dusty environment of its field operations. A completely axial flow compressor would have had very small and thin blades in the last stages of the compressor and thus be vulnerable to erosion by ingested sand resulting in performance degradation. These features were likely elements of the army proposal, and thus Stein must have been involved in its formulation. A later competitor to the Lycoming engine was produced by General Electric, with a more conventional configuration for the US Navy. In that application, sand ingestion would not be a problem!

CHAPTER 19

America

Arrival in New York. Furs coats were a thing then!

The weather was clear and cold as we approached New York harbor. We missed seeing the Statue of Liberty because we were on the right side of the ship, standing at the rails in awe of the view of the city and its skyscrapers. You could say we were on the starboard side looking at the port. We landed on Pier 76 of the United States Lines, watched the ship settle in, and descended the long gangplank to solid ground. The gathering of luggage and the dog, who was kenneled for the entire trip, took a little longer, but I don't remember it being any less than fairly quick. I suppose that first-class passengers must have gotten priority treatment.

We were picked up by Dr. Franz in what seemed like a huge car, where Mutti, the boys, and our dachshund Lumpi were settled in the back seat and Sig was in front. I remember the drive along the maze of limited access roads in New York, leading finally to the beautiful Hutchinson River and the Merritt Parkways to the city of Bridgeport in Connecticut. Stuck in my memory is the thumping of the tires as they crossed from one concrete pad to another on the latter highway constructed in the 1930s.

Bridgeport, at the time, was an important part of the industrial manufacturing world that was Connecticut more generally and showed itself to be all of that: a little rough around the edges. We obviously did not cruise the residential areas to get to the house that Dr. Franz had chosen for us. It was small and in a less-than-nice neighborhood, and Mutti was ready to go back to Germany right then and there. That first little rental house was a disappointing welcome to America.

Our first (*left*) and second (*right*) houses in America, together with our first American car

A little research into better housing solved the problem. Sig quickly set out to rent a place in the more residential town of Stratford. The new rental house was much nicer. It was a typical New England ranch-style home with a huge basement. It was located in a pleasant neighborhood with a big lawn and convenient to schools, shopping, and work. It was described in detail in a letter to the folks back in the old country, simply because America was so different.

The first business to be settled, according to the correspondence file, was the matter of travel expenses. The records show that a check was received for $3,025, which included about half that amount for four

Uli and Mutti shopping in the supermarket. Note that lard was readily sold, before the margarine industry gave the product a bad name! This photo was taken at the local A&P market on Main Street in Stratford, where I later had a summer job.

first-class tickets on SS *United States.* Freight for the shipment of goods amounted to about $500.

In the letter, Sig conveyed some interesting impressions of life in America. Cited as novelties were, among other things, houses constructed of wood, Venetian blinds, thermostat-controlled heating systems with automatic deliveries of heating oil by a fuel oil company, and built-in kitchen cabinets! There are also comments on food and supermarkets, the low price of gas and oil, the necessity of owning a car, American driving habits (slow), the necessity for credit establishment, convenient milk delivery, Wonder Bread ("Ugh!," he said. "Though not too bad when toasted"), and finally comments on school adjustments by the children. On the whole, he painted a happy picture of life here, emphasizing the Americans' friendliness and helpfulness in settling a new immigrant family.

Sig had learned French and English while in school, so he was somewhat prepared for the linguistic changes associated with the move. Mutti's language education was probably less intense, so she had to add to her new languages from a rustier standpoint. To her credit, she became competent after immersions in both languages, French and English, at the ages of forty-one and forty-nine, respectively. Quite an accomplishment!

The Jet Engine, Again

That first year, one of the patents whose ideas were originally developed at Junkers was granted on September 14, 1954, by the US Patent Office: 2,688,841 (with W. Stein) "Control device for gas turbine propulsion plants." It was filed on January 27, 1948, while Sig was working in France. An examination of the patent drawings (see a copy of cover page reproduced below) clearly shows the so-called onion as the flow controlling

In the Lycoming office: Sig, Adenstedt, and Franz, circa 1960. *Lycoming*

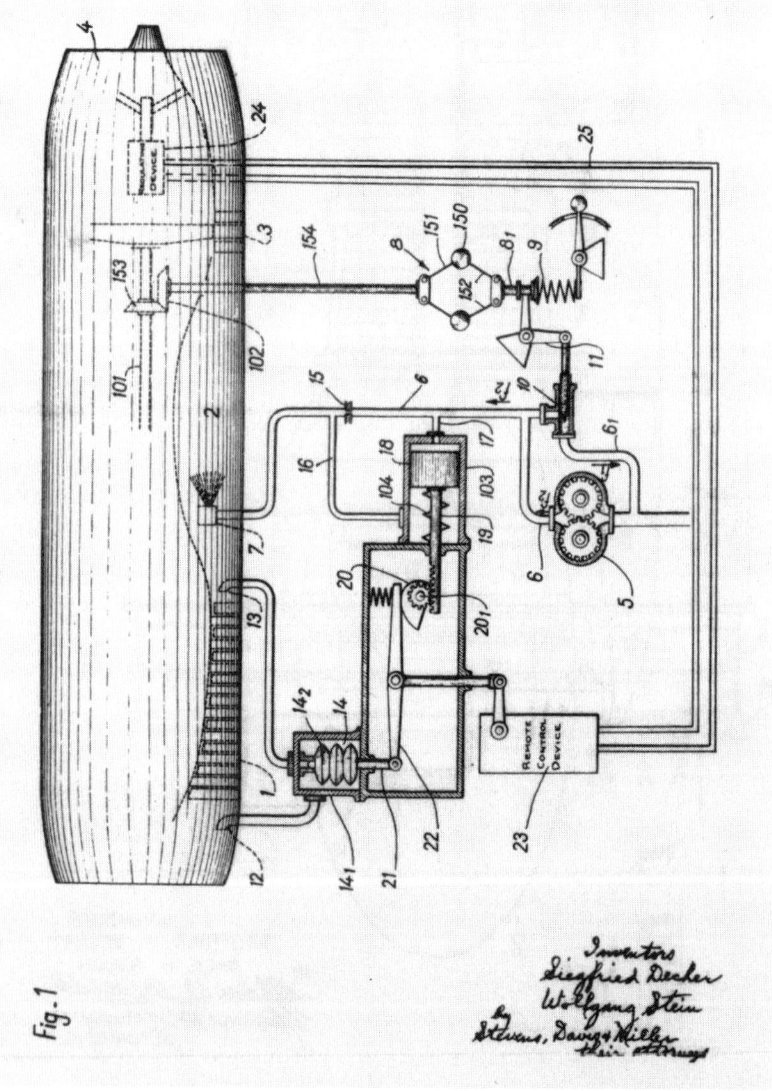
Sept. 14, 1954 S. DECHER ET AL 2,688,841

CONTROL DEVICE FOR GAS TURBINE PROPULSION PLANTS

Filed Jan. 27, 1948 5 Sheets-Sheet 1

The cover page for the American "onion" control system patent applied for while Sig was in France; it was awarded after our arrival in the United States.

device in the exhaust nozzle. Subsequently, this patent was often referenced in work done in the industry.

Looking in from the outside, it is hard to separate the specific work contributions of individuals within a corporate organization. AVCO-Lycoming indeed had a group of talented individuals who worked well together in the corporate setting. That setting included a small number of German engineers, as well as a significantly larger team of American engineers and people with other skills. Sig was doing well in the company. In 1957, he was promoted to Director of Research and Development, a position he maintained until retirement. The company enjoyed many successful engine projects that served its customers well. These gas turbine engines were primarily, but not exclusively, for helicopters. The most successful engines built by Lycoming were the T53 in the United States Army's Bell UH-1 (Huey) and the T55 in the Boeing Vertol CH-47 (Chinook). An examination of the workings of these engines reveals that these designers turned back, as seen from the perspective of the Jumo engine compressor, to the partial use of a *radial* flow compressor. The two engines have mixed *axial and radial* flow compressors.

The development of gas turbine engines in the industry led to ever-better-performing engines. The improvements in the efficiency of the compressor and blade cooling technology in the turbine pointed to larger amounts of power becoming available to the fan of fanjet engines that had been in service by the early 1960s. These fan jets enjoyed significant advantages over the simpler earlier generation of turbojet engines in that they were more fuel-efficient and quieter. The design aspect that describes the turbofan as such is the amount of air that bypasses the engine core. In the early turbofans, the bypass was about one to one, meaning that as much air is handled by the fan as the engine. This trend suggested to Sig that, rather than driving a fan handling about the same amount of air as through the burner and turbine, why not increase that flow to something much larger? In 1964, he wrote and presented a paper to the American Society of Mechanical Engineers on the topic. During this time, Lycoming had been quietly building and testing such an engine.

A patent application was filed with the US Patent Office on February 26, 1965, and granted as no. 3,390,527 (with Dale Rauch) on July 2, 1968, "High Bypass Ratio Turbofan." It was also granted in France and Great Britain.

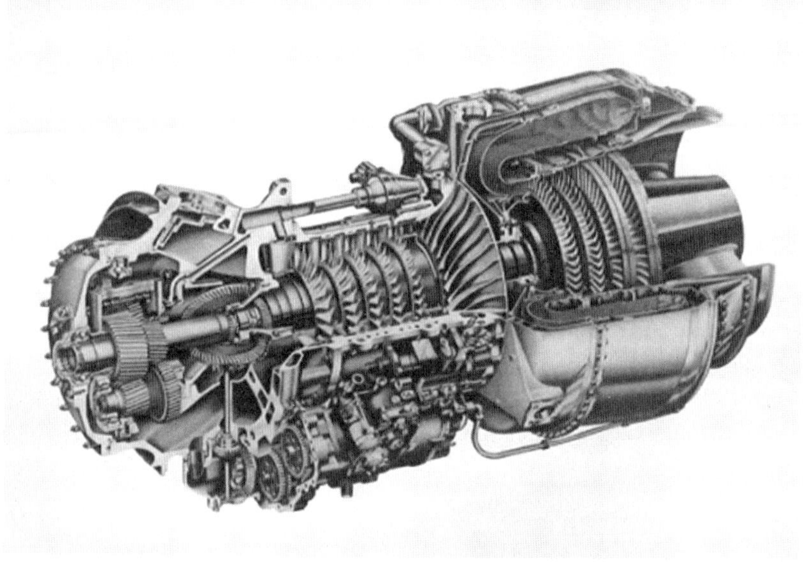

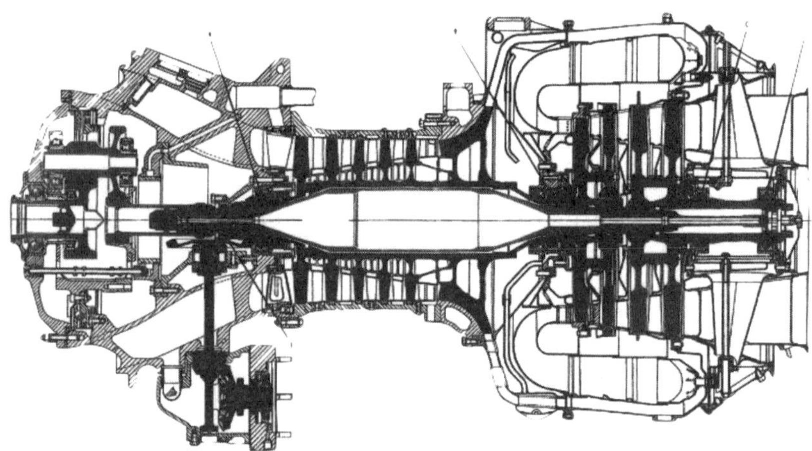

The Lycoming T53 turboshaft engine. The top illustration is a sectioned view (Lycoming), with the bottom image showing it in cross section (from a US Army training manual). The lines point out the engine's bearings. *Lycoming*

Author pointing to the "onion" flow control mechanism in a Jumo 004 engine on display at the Deutsches Technikmuseum Berlin

Franz, in his book *From Jets to Tanks: My Contribution to the Turbine Age,* suggests that the date of publication of the work related to the high bypass turbofan was in *Flight International* (magazine) in July 1963: "Lycoming Turbofans, First Details of the T55 Front-Fan Conversions." General Electric's work in that field was said to have been started in March 1964 and led to the large fan engines for the Lockheed C-5, built for the United States Air Force. The C-5 procurement also led directly to the Boeing Company turning their unfunded proposed airplane into the 747.

The bypass ratio of the Lycoming engine termed the PLF1A-2 had a very much larger fan flow rate relative to the engine. Its bypass ratio was 6:1. The prototype engine is on display at the Udvar-Hazy Center of the Smithsonian National Air and Space Museum in Washington, DC. The plaque describing the engine reads, in part:

> The high-bypass ratio turbine engine was benchmark technology because it offered higher takeoff thrust, lower fuel consumption,

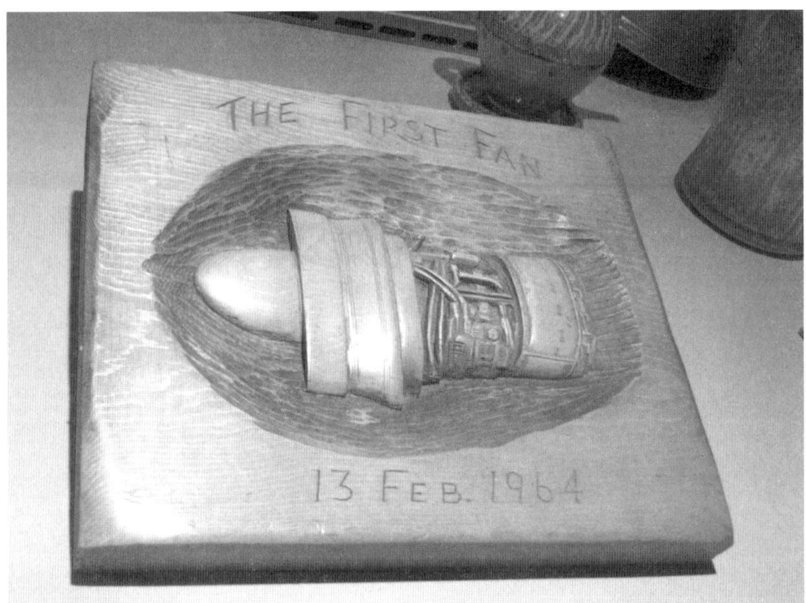

The front side of a wood carving presented to Sig on the occasion of his retirement in November 1977. The back reads: "The PLF1A-2 was the first high bypass turbofan to run on this continent. February 13, 1964, was a milestone for Lycoming and a triumph for Sig. Presented to S. Decher by Tony on November 18, 1977, so that he will always remember his friends in the Performance Dept."

> and quieter operation than other turbine engines. At Lycoming, concept studies began in the 1950s, and design of the PLF1A-2, one of two prototypes, began in 1962. The first test occurred two years later, when the PLF1A-2 became the first high-bypass turbofan engine to run in North America.
>
> The PLF1A-2 was never flown, but Lycoming used it to develop other engines including... the ALF 502, which powered Canadair Challenger CL600 executive jet and the British Aerospace Bae 146 commercial airliner.

The Smithsonian also prominently displays the Jumo 004 and a Whittle W.1 as the jet age's pioneering engines.

Examination of the patent drawing reveals that the Lycoming engineers were thinking in terms of relatively small engines because a mixed

The prototype Lycoming PLF1A-2 on display at the Udvar-Hazy Center of the Smithsonian National Air and Space Museum in Washington, DC, together with its descriptive plaque

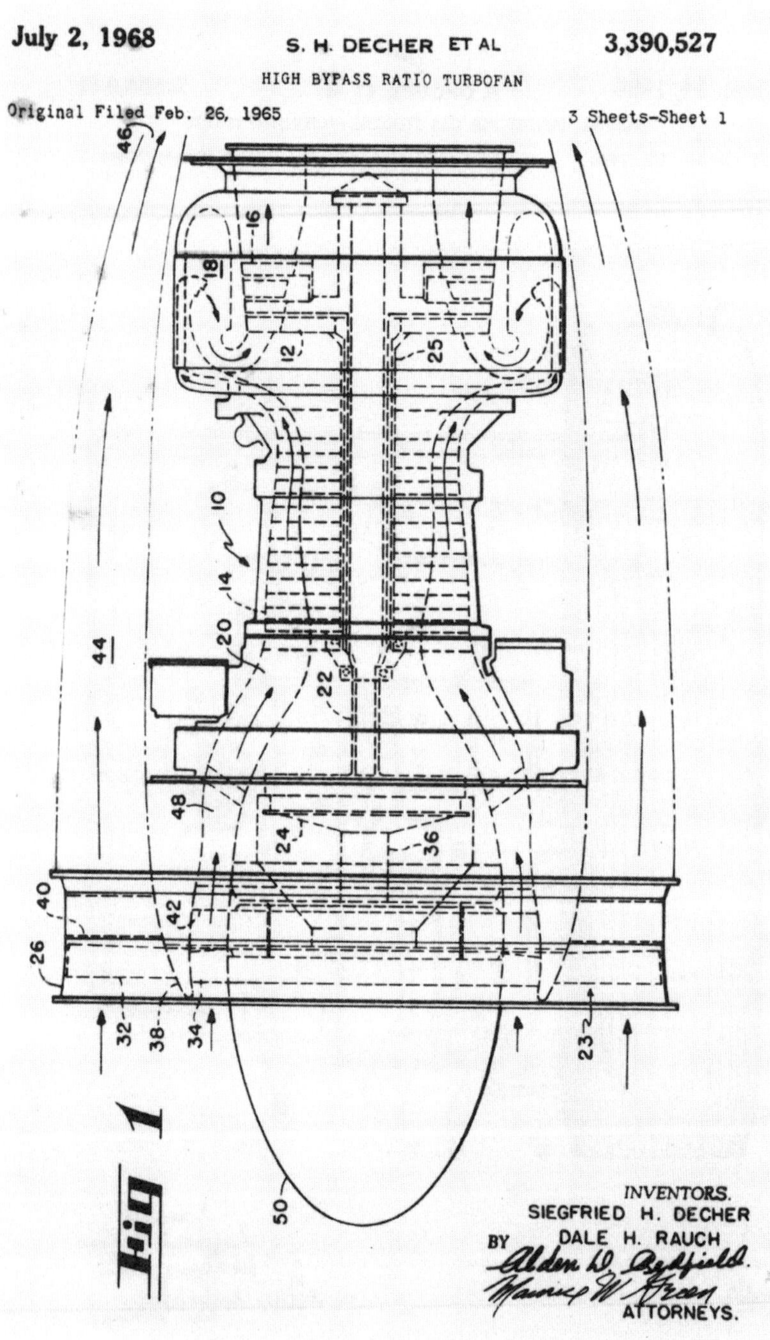

The cover page for the high bypass patent. Note the radial flow compressor stage and the reverse flow combustor also used in the T53 engine.

flow compressor is shown. The proof of concept demonstration used the Lycoming T55 as the core engine. The illustration in the patent application is very much an evolutionary design stemming from the T53, and the later, more powerful T55 engines that produce power on a shaft and not as jet power. Today, the principle of high bypass is employed in much larger engines, specifically in the engines that power every commercial jet airliner and military transport. These modern engines use purely axial flow compressors.

In the late 1960s, the high bypass engine concept was developed in the United States, by Pratt & Whitney and later General Electric, for the Boeing 747 (that first flew in 1969), and it made the design of the new generation of large airplanes with long ranges possible because of their high thrust and good fuel efficiency. The improvements allowed the design of long-range airplanes. It is hard to imagine the contrast from today to a time back to the late 1940s and early 1950s, when a transatlantic flight in a piston engine airplane often involved a refueling stopover along the way.

In the 1990s, the bypass ratio for the turbofan engine types grew even further, in a design sense, from about five to over ten, making the engines of that generation very powerful and efficient indeed. In addition, their very high degree of reliability allowed the use of only two engines for large airliners flying over large ocean reaches. To finish this discussion (and not as an afterthought), note that Rolls-Royce in Great Britain was and remains a world-renowned producer of these magnificent engines. In fact, Rolls-Royce teamed up with SNECMA (as did General Electric) to produce some of their engines. SNECMA (renamed "Safran") engines currently power many of the latest generations of Boeing and Airbus jets.

The picture (page 139) of the German engineering team that went from Junkers to Lycoming was taken in 1976. In broad terms, the roles these individuals played in the story are as follows. On American soil, Anselm Franz was the AVCO vice president who secured the US Air Force contract in 1952, assembled, and led the team. Heinz Möllmann was a specialist in control systems and worked closely with Sig. Heinrich Adenstedt was a metallurgist who probably had a hand in dealing with the challenges of the turbine cooling issues in the Jumo 004 and later acted as Franz's representative in matters related to assembling the

A high bypass turbofan engine on the wing of a Douglas DC-10 at Boeing Field in Seattle

Lycoming team. Friedrich Bielitz's technical expertise is not clear from the information in the files. He was probably a vibrations expert and he accompanied Franz and Adenstedt to the United States in 1945. His and Sig's relationship at Junkers must have been pretty close, as they traded a lot of correspondence regarding life in America.

The story of the engines that are the focus here is replete with missing details of the contribution of these team members under Franz, be they in Dessau or in Connecticut. A particular disappointment to this writer is that references to contributions by Wolfgang Stein cannot be found. Wolfgang Stein was the coauthor of the "onion" air flow control mechanism patent with Sig. It appears that he was involved in determining the engine configuration, while Sig's focus was the control system. Stein was also the originator of the Lycoming T53's reverse flow combustor. That design feature allowed the engine to be short and avoid the instability issues associated with a high-speed rotating shaft. While a thermodynamicist might be able to suggest the use of a regenerated gas

The individuals shown are, *left to right*, Adenstedt, Möllmann, Franz, Stein, Bielitz, and Decher. The picture also shows the axial flow compressor blading on the left and the burner. The single-stage turbine is under Sig's arm. This picture was taken in 1976 at the Lycoming plant, with the Jumo 004 engine on loan from the United States Air Force Museum in honor of the twenty-fifth anniversary of the Lycoming plant in Stratford, Connecticut. *Lycoming image C7506005-7*

turbine for an army tank, it also requires an expert in engine configurations to turn such ideas into a reality that meets performance, ruggedness, maintainability, and a myriad of other requirements for a practical engine. This task fell to Stein, and the acceptance by the US Army of the novel Lycoming (now Honeywell) AGT-1500 engine for the Abrams main battle tank speaks volumes to his skill.

This journey is described from the records and experiences of the author and his family. Sig was an engineer, as were his colleagues referenced above. As a rule, engineers do not leave records of the human and emotional part of life. There are no records of the arguments between members and avenues explored and not followed. That seems to be especially true for these engineers transplanted to a new country by the events of a devastating war. Sig, for one, was a very private man. He did not like to talk about his accomplishments, nor his setbacks. His setbacks were usually felt but not understood by our family. He kept his work experiences close and largely left them at the office. As I young adult, studied to be an engineer and became a member of the Aeronautics and Astronautics faculty at the University of Washington, where I was teaching the courses that Sig and I were both interested in. In retrospect, with vague feelings of disappointment, I recall that there was little dialogue about technical matters that we might have shared and explored together. There is always a gap between generations and that seems wider in people with European backgrounds than it might be for Americans. Consequently, I tell this story from rather thin records and from what can be learned by examining the industrial output of these engineers. The products they create are left to speak for themselves.

There are, of course, exceptions. Some engineers leave detailed historical records behind, of work done and tasks completed. As I grew to maturity in proximity to the Boeing Company, I mention here Bill Cook's story of "The Road to the 707" and the story "747" told by Joe Sutter. Considering how many engineers worked in the airplane industry (Boeing in particular) and how much they accomplished to allow the commercial deployment of very sophisticated aircraft, the ability to read about the detailed histories appears to be the exception.

No detailed records exist regarding the projects Sig was involved in. For some details, this story leans on the booklet written by Franz. In 1986, Dr. Franz sent me a copy, sure that I would be interested in it. I was indeed. It reflects what he accomplished yet includes no discussion of what it took to realize the various projects. His brief summary is a bit like a curriculum vitae, with only general details on the successful projects, some of which have been described here. The book was published as an internal document and printed by Lycoming, after Franz retired. To this reader, it seems like an attempt by Franz to leave something behind in order not to be forgotten. His technical achievements are remarkable, as were his management skills, but completely absent is the human component associated with traveling the difficult road he traveled so successfully. Franz must have been a very good manager, and he relied on the team of German and American engineers, to whom he gives credit by mentioning them as having been important. In what ways and for what specific contributions will, however, remain a mystery.

As a youngster, I met and became fairly well acquainted with Dr. Franz (and he was always Dr., even when Sig referred to him, as would have been culturally correct in Germany), at least as much as a teenager can come close to an "important" person. For a couple of high school summers, his son Peter and I spent a lot of time together at the Franz home, where a beach, a motorboat, and playful trouble were easy to find. These were always pleasant times in the beautifully modern Franz home. For Sig's retirement, Franz gave him a framed cross-section sketch of the Jumo 004 with the inscription:

> To my dear friend and old associate Siegfried,
> in remembrance of a great life of work together.
> 18. November 1977, Anselm Franz

The familiarity of that sentiment is gracious but surprising to the author. The closeness of the German engineers in their work did not translate into close family/friendly social relations. As engineers, their social nuclei were their families. There were occasional social interactions, but they were rare. My brother and I, as well as the children of the other German engineers, were teenagers in the United States, where social events would customarily include the children, but the interactions were quite formal.

I cannot recall any events of the type I have known in my own American life where parties or meals among the German engineers were shared for social connectivity. The reasons may have to do with being German, immigrants, engineers, or simply happy without them.

CHAPTER 21

Americanization

A dimension of adapting to a new culture is fitting in linguistically. Sig was fluent in English albeit with a German accent. In the industrial environment where the dominant part of his use of the English language was plied, the language had a certain roughness in that swear words were rather commonly used. The words "damn" and "sh*t" come up as normal expressions of frustration or some other emotion. These same words are also common in the German language so that, to be au courant, all Sig had to do was use them as he would in German. There are differences, however, in the cultural acceptance of the word sh*t and the German equivalent, "Scheisse." In German, the word is less strong than it is in American English and seems to be less of a reference to the substance the word describes.

One fine day, the circumstances of which I cannot remember, I had a chance to listen to Sig, expounding in English with those delicate words sprinkled in his vocabulary. I had become aware of the fact that, in the US, use of these words was a sign of less than gentlemanly stature or upbringing. That exposure led to an evening discussion of the subject wherein I suggested he avoid their use because it sounds particularly rough, especially when delivered with a foreign accent. He understood the argument and never used them again. At home, where the lingua franca was German, even when strong feelings were in play, he rarely resorted to their use. The young can teach the elder!

With work going well and with the recommendation that Sig buy a house because it was a good investment, he went for that option. He bought a lot in Trumbull, Connecticut, close to Pinewood Lake, which provided swimming and canoeing in the summer and ice skating in the winter. Over the summer of 1955, our family cleared the lot with hand tools—no chainsaws—always ending the day at Dairy Queen. He contracted the construction of a very modern (prefabricated) Techbuilt house that was quite a luxury for us. The children finished high school in that house, while Sig occupied his weekends building stone walls and making many improvements to the place.

In 1961, our entire immediate family became US citizens.

Sig and Mutti enjoyed their home, with us children and with Lumpi, the dog. This family companion started life in Decize and later barked in what appears to have been English. The family led a pretty normal, quiet life. Evenings might find Sig playing a guitar or, more often, an accordion. Mutti always did the cooking and carved the meat in the kitchen, as was the German tradition, and we boys did the dishes. Social interactions with neighbors were limited to Sig's smile and always greeting people with a handshake. A measure of this wish for not being noticed in the larger world seems to have been reflected in his choice of cars. Until the last decade of his life, he always drove a car built in the country where he lived.

Settling in America meant that local customs had to be considered and understood. One I recall involved a booklet he read while still in Germany about the fact that in American communities, people were strongly tied to and involved with a church. After he settled in the home we built in Trumbull, he joined a local protestant church and paid tithes to it. He probably went to the church just once and to sign up and register us boys for confirmation. My brother and I went to church service during that period and completed the confirmation process. This was around the time when I went off to college, and I never returned to the church. Sig's connection to it came to an amusing end around a scandal involving the pastor's infidelity portrayed in the newspaper. Subsequently, Sig was asked to increase his church contribution "commensurate with his status and income." He responded by terminating his membership in the congregation he really never knew. It appears he learned that church participation was not nearly as much of a requirement for life in the United States as he had read about or as his mother had hoped.

My brother and I eventually left for college and returned in the summer to work various jobs. Mine were primarily at Sikorsky Aircraft in the Preliminary Design group, which was a wonderful introduction to working in industry. In time, we moved permanently to new cities and married.

Sig saw that education was the key to the professional life he so enjoyed. He was consequently a strong supporter of education for his two boys, and we gratefully benefitted from that largesse. By the time I went to college, it was the time of Sputnik, and the pursuit of education in the field of engineering was encouraged by both Sig and the country as a whole. It was a mighty wave to ride, and I enjoyed it all the way to retirement.

When Sig retired from Lycoming on a festive occasion in November 1977, he had the title of "Director of Research and Development." I have a number of pieces of memorabilia given to Sig at the retirement party, including a wood carving of his turbofan engine (see figure on page 134). Judging from candid photographs, the event was attended by many, including Mutti and Uli and his wife. Colleagues from Sig's university

The Stratford Army Engine Plant in 2011

days in Germany were there, as well as many professional contacts who enjoyed working with him. Of course, Franz was in attendance, for whom Sig was a technical right-hand man for more than two decades. I was notably absent, as my wife and I who were living on the West Coast and in the middle of the academic semester, and could not make the trip. In my note to Papa, I mentioned also being in the middle of a house remodeling project and that I expected Sig and Mutti to visit in the near future. I cannot recall whether a visit did take place the following year, but I do know that Papa and Mutti came out in the summer of 1979, where we ended up seeing the summer wildflowers at Hart's Pass in the Cascade Mountains.

In retirement, Papa and Mutti eventually moved to a less maintenance-intensive home. There, he began to experience a series of health setbacks. Mutti was convinced that the war years as well as the stresses associated with work came to haunt him with a heart attack, then a stroke, both of which he survived. A second heart attack from which he was expected to recover was his last. Mutti spoke sadly of his stay in a two-person room at Bridgeport Hospital, where his roommate continuously watched what he considered idiotic television. It might have been too much for him. He desperately wanted quiet rest and did not get it.

I am quite certain that all the engineers in this story have passed away. My father Sig died in January 1980. Mutti died five years later, to the day. Both could look back on their lives as well lived under sometimes difficult and sometimes joyful circumstances.

AVCO-Lycoming was eventually sold and resold. On a visit in 2016, the parking lot in Stratford, Connecticut, was empty with rusty, leaning fences surrounding acres of asphalt. Weeds in the cracks where thousands of workers once parked and built Lycoming engines betray a kind of historical abandonment.

CHAPTER 22

Following in His Footsteps

My late teen years were heavily influenced by my father. I must have consulted with him often while he was in the office because I remember his extension number vividly: 569. As it was to me, it may be interesting to the reader to better understand what led me to follow in the footsteps of a very able engineer within what was often a complicated relationship between father and son. A few paragraphs may add to an understanding of the complexities involved in our generational differences, differences in social culture, and the personal experiences described above.

The transition to American life necessarily involved learning English. Having two languages already under control made learning a third one rather rapid (intimidating and not necessarily painless). There were a lot of vocabulary similarities with the languages I knew, but the pronunciation was not easy or intuitive. I recall being seated in a junior high school class, after arriving in America just two months earlier. I was given a book to read, and after I made it clear with the teacher that I was lost, she said in so many words, "Well, just sit there," while the class carried on. The book opened to text and pictures of early western exploration of the American continent with a display of a "dugout canoe." I thought, *Let's see, "dugout" appears to be a French word, and how should I pronounce the "e" at the end of "canoe"?* The mysteries of language were everywhere!

Interactions with other students were limited, but they were curious about this "strange" kid who joined them halfway through the year. I did not dress in blue jeans, for example, because they were not part of the wardrobe we brought from Europe. Shopping for a new one to set in motion an external metamorphosis in order to appear American was definitely not high on my parents' priority list! There were many other aspects of the adjustment to America that had to be mastered, but by the end of the school year, my English competence had improved markedly. My summer was well spent with American kids and television at their houses, and progress was smooth and steady.

A major interest I brought with me from France and Germany was my love for model trains. Thanks to birthdays and Christmases, I had built up a sizeable collection of rolling stock and track, and I continued building the set in the huge basement of the Stratford rental house and later in Trumbull. Additions to the collection required trips to a small shop in Bridgeport that fortunately included my brand of AC-powered Märklin HO railroadiana. Conveniently, a bus line to the city went through Stratford right past our house. I used it to frequent the hobby shop. Because I always sat near to front of the bus to see where we were going, I got to know a driver on the route. I must have piqued his interest sufficiently to engage me in conversation. He was probably curious about my accent and my background, and I was interested in learning more about my new world. It was a chance for this fourteen-year-old to talk English to an adult. Thus, I boarded his orange and grey GMC bus on a number of occasions and always sat over the right front wheel, admired the amazing (and new to me) automatic transmission, and talked with this wonderful and interesting man while we cruised the city. He shared his driving schedule with me so that he could be my driver when I chose to go into town. Sometimes I went to ride the bus just for the tour, not headed for the hobby shop. On those after-school journeys, there were only a few other passengers getting on and off now and then, so the conversation was easy. He would explain things, and I would listen and ask questions. After a short and interesting break at the bus base, where I was treated to a soda, we returned to the route and back home. I don't remember much about the man, except for his friendly engagement with me. Seen from today's perspective, there is certainly the possibility that one might suspect nefarious motives. But the times were different, and there was no reason that my mother should have worried (and didn't) for my being gone for an afternoon of cruising the industrial city of Bridgeport. Americans were warm and welcoming. Access to the hobby store in Bridgeport broadened my hobby world with exposure to plastic models of modern American military airplanes, of which I made many.

By the end of that summer, my transition to English was complete, save perhaps for a small hard-to-detect accent. As I entered high school in Stratford that fall, I was amazed that the people I talked to did not suspect that I was a language newbie. My name might have given it away, for I chose to remain "Reiner," in contrast to having been "René," when we were living in France. I did not care for "Ronald." The accent issue came up again later, just once, when I started teaching at the University of Washington, when a student in my very first class asked me:

"Are you Canadian?"

I told him I was not. I was probably a little nervous. I was also asked, incredulously, "Are *you* the professor?"

I admitted that I was. I suppose that when one is a young twenty-nine-year-old, there is a certain shortage of credibility!

My time in America, starting with my high school years, set me up to rapidly become an American. Television had a great deal to do with this process of Americanization, as did the pop music of the mid-1950s. Sig adjusted to the new world on a somewhat more modest path by largely ignoring the television and the radio music I preferred. He was busy with his work and wanted to do it well by focusing on it. Sig was, in my mind, a laissez-faire father but a devoted head of the family. That meant the child management was left to Mutti, and she was good at it. There were, however, times when he would step in with strong objections to certain decisions.

A television of our own came up early as an issue, when we lived in our rental house in Stratford and we boys spent a lot of time with the neighborhood kids watching TV at their houses. Sig did not see it as important, and we disagreed, of course. I claim that it was a big component of my learning English. Generally speaking, the TV English was clear, accent-free, and the meaning of words mostly obvious. My brother's and my keen interests in the medium soon led to lobbying for a set of our own, which was our big Christmas present that first year. It was relegated to a bedroom, and it definitely was *not* the centerpiece of our living room. In both our rental house and later in the Trumbull house, the living room housed Sig's desk and a good radio for listening to WQXR, the *New York Times* classical music station, while he worked or paid bills.

While I can say that we were not heavy TV watchers, my brother and I took in the prime time shows of the day, as well as some age-appropriate entertainment. The latter included *Lassie, Roy Rogers, Lone Ranger,* and the like. On primetime shows, we saw quiz shows, dramas like the *General Electric Theater* hosted by Ronald Reagan, the *Ed Sullivan Show,* and more. One of the more memorable series I watched was *Victory at Sea,* recounting the battles of World War II in the Pacific. Neither parent spent much time with us watching the small black and white screen, nor was there much discussion about what we watched. Television was the new form of storytelling I enjoyed. When we were living in Decize, I recall many an hour sitting by the radio with its green tuning eye, listening to the audio stories broadcast by Radio Luxembourg.

In spite of my rapid Americanization, my high school experiences were those of an immigrant. I was not part of the social scene but participated in activities such as running the movie projectors for classes

The Trumbull house

that needed them and distributing the *New York Times* to civics classes every morning. Academically, I did well. This rests in part on having had a lot of the math and science exposure in France, where it was taught earlier than in the United States. Seeing this material a second time made it much easier to pass my exams. Another dimension of my academic success was that American public education imposes rather light (compared to French or German schools) expectations on its students. It is relatively easy for an American student to shine if one is determined to do so or if one's parents have strong expectations. The latter applied in my case.

My brother and I augmented our science education with extracurricular involvement in the chemical aspects of rocket fuel concoctions and investigations of interesting chemical reactions, the metal mercury, and such. A nearby abandoned airfield allowed us to test the rockets we built, most of them unsuccessfully, but there was always fire and noise involved. Reality had a way of correcting our understanding of physics, and fortunately, injuries were never involved. The smells and noises from our quarters wafting through the house would have alarmed me if I had been the parent!

My good grades in the subjects I knew set me up for a career in engineering. My necessary competence in English as a language took about six months to develop. Understanding or developing talent in American sports, where I was a complete novice, took longer—actually much longer. The subtleties of baseball and American football will always remain a bit of a mystery to me. My high school yearbook suggests that I must have made a good impression on some of my classmates. The fact that Mutti thwarted any rapid Americanization by keeping me from wearing blue jeans did not seem to have been an insurmountable impediment.

Summers in Connecticut were good times spent in a neighborhood full of kids our ages. The nearby lake offered canoeing (I knew how to pronounce the word by then), swimming, and, at home, helping with mowing the lawn and chores. The summer before I turned sixteen, I took my first job assisting with program distribution for the new Shakespeare theater in Stratford—not upon-the-Avon, but in Connecticut! It was probably at the suggestion of Miss Paris, my Stratford High School history teacher, that this opportunity arose. Because I was underage, I could not be paid but was given an opening night ticket to see *Julius Caesar* starring well-known actors and well attended by the New York theater crowd. Attendance at other plays in the summers that followed developed my lifelong love of plays by the Bard. Later, my paid summer jobs included bagging groceries at the local A&P supermarket and working for a catering outfit offering picnics and fancy meals at party events like weddings. Here I became very familiar with American food and loved the clean-up sessions after large events, sometimes taking place after midnight. The other young employees and I often ate (the leftovers) like kings! Sprinkled into this were a new driver's license and the discovery of girls.

With high school coming to an end, it was time to think about my expected path of going to college. Sig and I did a tour of New England schools that were candidates, but all options included a pathway to engineering. Schools considered were liberal arts colleges that had combination programs with an engineering school and schools with only engineering and science as curricular themes. On this trip, Sig's degree of assimilation into Americana was revealed one evening as we stayed in a motel near Middlebury College in Vermont. The local movie theater was playing the musical *South Pacific*, which I wanted to see. We took our seats in the theater, but Sig did not have whatever it took to watch the show to the end. I was never able to know the answer to the question "Why?," but there was no arguing the point. There rarely ever was. On my own and at another time, I enjoyed all of the show in its entirety.

Of the colleges I applied for, I chose to attend the most expensive of the options. Sig did not balk. The $800 per semester tuition for Rensselaer Polytechnic Institute in upstate New York was high, but he accepted my choice. Obviously, he quietly drew satisfaction from my seeking an educational path in engineering.

Since Sig was an engineer, it would have made sense that I would gain positive feedback, or at least an expression of acceptance, for my decision. Indeed, he allowed me to proceed in following his footsteps, but this was without ever engaging me in discussions of our shared subject matter. He could have taken an interest in what I was learning, and better yet, he could have shared some of the challenges and issues of interest in his work. But he didn't. There was this ever-present old

Europe versus new America culture gap. I suppose it can also be argued that Sig's approach was to enable me to reach my goals without interfering with them and thereby having to accept responsibility for them. Another explanation for his lack of involvement in my education might have been that his upbringing did not include a father as a role model, since he lost his at age eleven. To be fair, however, I am sure he had a hand in my obtaining a job at Lycoming when I turned eighteen. I spent that summer as an assistant technician in the metallurgical laboratory, testing the crystal structure of turbine blades. We used nasty mixtures of hydrochloric acid and hydrogen peroxide—interesting work, but hard on exposed skin!

Later in life, given my interests, I suppose I could have chosen to pursue a career in construction, architecture, or linguistics. The law would not have been an option, because the children in Sig's presence were not (I could say never) allowed to engage in healthy arguments.

In family matters, Sig had a fairly rigid mindset. Differences in opinion or conflict were often settled by Mutti, who engaged him in private at a later time to resolve the issue by promoting an understanding of the boys' viewpoint(s). Two significant and memorable events along this pattern will forever stick in my mind. One had to do with spending my own money, saved from part-time and summer work, to buy a red MGA sports car. The summer work I was engaged in at the time was at Sikorsky Aircraft. I was a third-year student at Rensselaer, at the age of twenty-one, and in Sig's eyes, I was still just an immature young man. I felt it was time I had wheels of my own. To put it mildly, Sig thought it made more sense to have a nice sedate little sedan. (Why? . . . To attract girls?)

"Nur Angeber fahren so'n Auto!!" ("Only show-offs would drive a car like that!"), he would say about the new red convertible in the driveway.

With Mutti's help, I prevailed.

Another dramatic event occurred when I moved into a fraternity house in my second year of college. The reader can probably imagine what kind of dwelling this was, but it was what I wanted, and that's where my friends were. I lost the argument for an entire fall semester, when I was made to live in a room of an ivy-covered dormitory on campus. Very embarrassing! Sig was paying the bills, however! Here, again, Mutti spoke on my behalf when they were alone and said to him: "Just keep an eye on his grades." He reluctantly gave in and allowed me to choose as I became my own person. Parenting is tough, and so is growing up.

Strangely, Sig's interest in my work was almost nonexistent all through later life as well. His measure of contentment seems to have rested on my milestones and satisfaction that they were reached. I am sure he drew a good deal of satisfaction from having steered both his boys to educational levels of achieving doctoral degrees, me in aeronautical engineering and my brother in nuclear engineering. For me, the distance aspect of my father-son relationship was difficult, and I was determined to be different in raising my own children. Their academic interests, though different from mine, did not inhibit my interest in their schoolwork, especially when math or sciences were the challenge at hand.

The summer before Sig died, he and Mutti came to Seattle to visit us and enjoy the Northwest mountains he grew to love. One of the activities of the stay was a trip into the high Cascades to enjoy the mountain air and the views afforded by a short hike along flowered trails through alpine meadows. Sig enjoyed photography, and wildflowers were a special love. The camera he took on that trip ended up in my possession after he died that winter.

My first use of it was to document a training session for a climb of Mount Rainier later that season. A friend and I introduced a group of six novice climbers to the notion of camping on snow and acquainting them with the basics of mountain safety—crevasse rescue most specifically. The date of the trip was the weekend of May 17–18, 1980. After spending the night at 7,000 feet elevation on the south side of the mountain above the Nisqually Glacier, it was time to eat breakfast and prepare for the day's activity. It was a nice morning with high, thin clouds that a warming sun would surely drive away.

While eating breakfast and watching teams of climbers plodding toward higher places on the mountain, we heard someone yell out, "Look at Mt. St. Helens!" We turned and saw the mountain that had been visible, now involved in a cloud of eruptive material bursting upward. Near us, we heard rocks fall from high places, but otherwise, it was quiet. Our day was going to be changed. A violent eruption had taken place, the first in a century in the lower forty-eight states. Everything stopped, and we viewed in awe the eruption cloud quickly rising above the thin cloud layer. Some of us wondered whether the volcano on whose flanks we stood might somehow be connected to the structure of Mt. St. Helens. It wasn't. We were 40 miles away. Four minutes after the eruption, a loud boom reached us, a manifestation of the speed of sound and the distance it had to cover to reach us. Sig's camera was put to good use and documented the events of the day.

For more than two hours we were transfixed, but we knew that we were going to miss the lessons of the day and headed home. The high cloud of ash was headed our way. We packed up as lapilli, small aggregated lumps of ash, rained softly on us as if we were in a summer storm. The droplets exploded into little puffs of dust, and soon ash dust was everywhere. It was time to go, and it was getting darker. When packing up the tents, it was white underneath, and the snow next to them was black with wet lapilli dust!

When we reached the Paradise Lodge parking lot, we were surprised to see an image inversion of an almost white dusted road surface and black, moistened ash-covered snowbanks. The previous warm sunny day, the pavement was black and the snowbanks were white. We drove out of the park in pitch blackness. The slippery road was covered with half an inch of volcanic ash. Following other cars closely was impossible from a visibility viewpoint because of the volcanic dust, making the exit from the now-closed park time-consuming. After we reached clear air, I had the oil changed in the old VW bus to avoid engine damage for having driven through a "severe dust storm" of the volcanic kind.

My wife, Mary, was not part of this excursion. She did not need the training, as we had previously climbed Rainier and some of the other Cascades volcanoes. She would like to have been with us but also felt the need to stay home with our two preteen daughters. Hearing a boom, she nevertheless experienced the eruption looking out the kitchen window at the family horse that was grazing on the back lawn. The very rapid seismic wave through the ground and the associated boom apparently reached the horse right then. She did a kind of four-legged crow hop from a munching position, looked around, and went back to munching. "What was that about?" The news broadcasts cleared up the situation.

The slides that came from the camera were of great interest to everyone. I was pulled into a university community of people with similar experiences and pictures. A few days later, the largest auditorium on the campus of the University of Washington was filled twice for slide shows for the curious.

Development of the film in the camera also revealed Sig's last photographs: lupine, Indian paintbrush, larkspur, and other mountain wildflowers, all taken on that trip to Hart's Pass the previous summer. On this last day "together," we shared our love for the beauty of nature, even if we could not share our interest in the work that we both enjoyed.

EPILOGUE

When Sig died in 1980, no one had any idea that 1989 would bring a tidal change to the political world that affected, among many places, the land where he started his professional career. The chaos imposed on Germany by the Cold War on an already chaotic state of affairs after the end of a hot world war was about to be undone. Had he lived, he would have followed the events in Germany and the collapse of the Soviet Union with interest because it opened possibilities for revisiting the places where he left footprints during the war. While he could not and did not visit the former East Germany (a.k.a. DDR), I could and did.

In order to know Germany and to understand a bit better what it means to have been German, I made a number of journeys to the country of my birth. My first extensive trip was a sabbatical in connection with my academic work in the United States. I applied for and was granted a Fulbright Visiting Professorship at the University of Karlsruhe in the early 1980s. I got to know Germany and improve my German beyond that of a thirteen-year-old. The East was off-limits. Fortunately, in the years 1998–99, I had a second Fulbright, this time at the Technical University of Berlin. The wall had fallen a decade earlier, and that afforded me a firsthand look at the transformation of a land and people that had been chained by an autocracy of devastating proportions. Naturally, I visited the place where I was born, Dessau, and the locale of the Junkers factory where Sig worked. It was a strange feeling to have been standing in a place where, in the past, I would have been afraid.

On a later occasion, I took time to see what was left of the Junkers factory. There was a museum open, paying homage to what Junkers did. The display of the man's work focused heavily on gas-powered water heaters that were widely used in Germany and a little of his airplane work. The factory's work after he died centered on military airplanes that played a devastating role in the war. Junkers, the man, would have been devastated. The museum was little more than a collection of stuff laid out on tables, with improvements forthcoming as funding allowed. There was little to see regarding the jet engine that Sig helped build. I was told that most of the engineering work was done in a so-called Mader building, several blocks away. The building was partially rebuilt after bomb damage, and a visit there did not shine much light on its history.

In front of the museum were wind tunnels, shells of flaking concrete, not likely to ever be used again. No museum in the former DDR, including the Junkers, is (at least it was then) complete without a display of a few tired Soviet military jets, MiGs, and the like, which have outlived their usability and role. There was a lot of concrete surfacing, as there always is at airfields, with weeds growing in the cracks. I would have enjoyed walking these streets with Sig, watching his reactions, and letting him reminisce.

While I could wax endlessly on experiences in Germany, particularly in Berlin, during that Fulbright year, I will resist, except to note that my experience at that time was thoroughly enriched by a young man who worked in the laboratory where I was working. He grew up in the walled city and knew it well. As a young lad, he witnessed some of Berlin's Cold War history, including spy exchanges while watching from a safe distance in the woods. He and his playmates made a sort of game of short-circuiting the military exercises involving red and blue teams of American soldiers who would rather have been in warm barracks than miserable in pup tents in the Berlin woods. The boys knew the woods and the disposition of the training teams, and relayed important information that shortened the time required for their exercises... in trade for chocolate.

Every Wednesday, he and I took long walks to explore corners of the city that tourists did not know about or could not find. The physical reminders of Nazi times and the idiosyncratic artifacts associated with the city's division were thought provoking. They reflect a certain degree of lunacy in human endeavors, such as wall building, checkpoints, courageous escapes, tyranny, want, and so on. In time, they will vanish, but should they not remind us to do better?

I conclude with a story about Otto Lilienthal, the aviation pioneer mentioned earlier in our story in connection with the list of organizations where Sig once was a member. It seems that the East German airline Interflug had an old Ilyushin Il-62 airliner that was going to be scrapped because of its many flight hours. The people in the town of Stölln in the East German state of Brandenburg were justly proud of their townsman Lilienthal and felt that the hill on which he did his gliding experiments needed something special to remember him by. The site had changed since his flying days, when he had his fatal accident, but there was a 3,000-foot grass field still in use for modern gliders. The citizens of Stölln learned about the fate of the airliner and talked the airline as well as the DDR authorities into letting them permanently display it at the field as a tribute to the man and the modern state of aviation.

An Il-62 normally takes about 7,500 feet of concrete runway to land, so the task of bringing it in was indeed a challenge, if not dangerously crazy. With calculations made that showed the possibility of doing this, they tried and succeeded to land the airplane on the grass field. The thrust reversers needed for stopping processed a good deal of the sod, somewhat obscuring the actual event on the videos available on the internet. The soil processed by the engines surely rendered the engines beyond repair, but the airframe was unscathed. This event took place on October 23, 1989. The political unrest in East Germany at this time brought the Berlin Wall down on November 9 of that year, just two weeks later.

The DDR will not be missed, especially its State Security system, the Stasi, which relied on everybody spying on everybody else. Yes, these were the agents of a government that shot its citizens for attempting to leave the terror and economic dead-end when they tried to climb over the wall. *Republikflucht* (or "flight from the republic") was a crime. DDR officials also periodically cleared traffic from the Autobahn north of Berlin where they lived, so that they could run their fancy Volvos and other Western cars at high speeds while supposedly unobserved and unencumbered by the few people who had to drive miserable little "Trabis." The Trabant was a small car with a 25-horsepower, two-cycle engine, the subject of much ridicule by people in the West when the wall fell, crumbled, and evaporated.

What if... ? As I watched the reunification of Germany after the immediate events of the autumn of 1989, it does occur to me to wonder what life might have been like had Sig not been the man he was and not made the decisions he did. There is, of course, the matter of political freedom and the opportunities I was able to exploit because I grew into adulthood in America. The consequences of the *Wende* (the "change," as Germans call the reunification events) were as dramatic for the people who lived in the East as the consequences experienced by Western Germans during currency reform in 1948. The economic consequences for the ordinary DDR citizens (which is what they considered themselves to be, not Germans) was a very favorable exchange of a nearly worthless currency for a hard one that the German D-Mark was. Many of the new DMs were quickly spent on bananas (a forbidden fruit in the DDR) and on modern cars, which were, as it turned out, short-term and, not surprisingly, quickly depreciating investments. In the period that followed, the many VEBs (*Volkseigener Betrieb*, or "people-owned enterprises") were put on sale to be privatized and gobbled up by people with a longer-term outlook who sensed a profit opportunity. How would I have fared in the turmoil that still extends into the future that is the present day? It Is impossible to say, of course, but the mind does wonder. I do feel fortunate in ways that defy description.

Today, should you pay a visit to modern Germany, the Lilienthal memorial Il-62 in Stölln has been beautified and is open. You can even arrange for a wedding to take place on board!

Appendixes

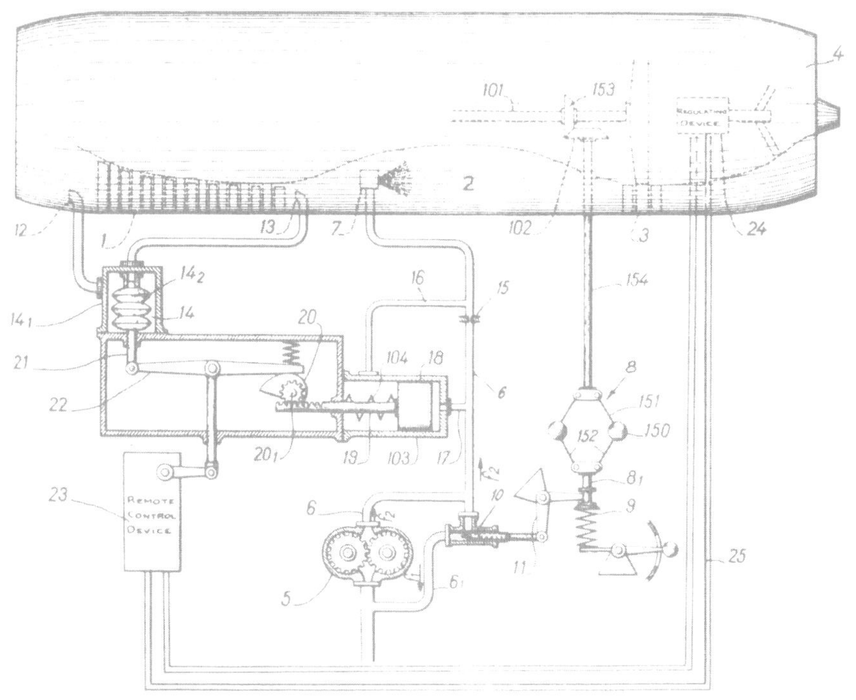

APPENDIX 1
German Patents

The following is a partial list of patent awards to Siegfried Decher. Others are cited where they arise in the story. These patents are secured by the Junkers company. They are listed by date with a short summary. The titles are in German with translation.

May 22, 1944. Notification from Junkers patent office that a patent (Geschwächte Schaufelprofilspitze [Reduced sharpness blade leading edge] A. 1808/E.57/43) applied for on March 26, 1943, was granted.

May 25, 1944. Notification from Junkers patent office that a patent (Axialverdichter Fühlsteurung [Axial compressor flow (?) control]/1764) applied for on March 11, 1942, was granted.

September 1, 1944. Notification from Junkers patent office that a patent (Überkritisch ausströmendes TL-Gerät [Supercritical nozzle device; TL refers to jet engine]/1771/375) applied for on March 3, 1943, was granted.

For each of the three of the above patents, a monetary award of fifty Reichsmarks was made.

There was an inquiry made by Sig to Junkers and their patent office in Mainz (Western Zone) about the maintenance of his patents. The response (dated September 11, 1950) states that his request for maintaining a number of patent documents at Junkers' cost was denied. He was, however, invited to maintain them at his own expense. The reason given is that they have been overtaken by newer technology, or will be in the near future—a future wherein an application in Germany is unlikely because of the economic and military situation. He replies, agreeing with the assessment, and returned the original files. The deadline for patent renewal was to be September 30, 1950.

APPENDIX 2
Zeugnisse

The word *Zeugnis* translated means "testimony." In the German professional circles inhabited by Sig, it was (and probably still is) customary for an employer to write a letter about the work and character of the subject. The following pages are such testimonies given by officials at Junkers—two by SNECMA and one by ILO. I believe that the letter by Prof. Triebnigg was in connection with his and Sieg's close technical collaboration. He was also a close personal friend of Sig's. His title as professor reveals that he had left SNECMA sometime before Sig did and had landed an academic position in Germany, which was beginning to restart its institutions. Prof. Triebnigg was not alone in leaving France for German academic positions. There were several others in the Decize group who did the same.

JUNKERS FLUGZEUG- UND -MOTORENWERKE
AKTIENGESELLSCHAFT
MOTORENBAU
STAMMWERK DESSAU

Oberursel, 26. Juni 1945

Zwischenzeugnis

Herr Dipl.-Ing. Siegfried D e c h e r , geboren am 2.11.1912 in Darmstadt, ist am 15.8.1936 als Versuchsingenieur in die Abteilung Sonderaufgaben unserer Flugmotoren-Entwicklung eingetreten.

Neben kleineren Versuchskonstruktionen hat er zunächst umfangreiche theoretische Untersuchungen zur Klärung der Ausströmverhältnisse bei Zünderflugmotoren als Grundlage zur Berechnung des Abgasschubes bei Freiauspuff und die dazu erforderlichen Indizierversuche selbständig durchgeführt. Daneben hat er durch Flugversuche mit der Ju 87 Unterlagen über das Höhenverhalten des Abgasschubes geschaffen. Arbeiten auf dem Gebiet der Gebläseentwicklung und Versuche und theoretische Untersuchungen zur Bestimmung der Verlustleistungen bei Zündermotoren gaben ihm einen solchen Überblick über das Leistungsverhalten von Flugmotoren, daß wir ihm die Vorausberechnung der Höhenleistung, die Leistungs-Projektierung neuer Motorenmuster und die Leitung der betreffenden Arbeitsgruppe übertragen konnten.

Mit dem Beginn der Entwicklung des Turbinen-Luftstrahl-Triebwerkes haben wir ihm neben den genannten Aufgaben die Leistungsauslage, die Durchführung der mit thermodynamischen Fragen zusammenhängenden Versuche dieses neuen Gerätes und die Bearbeitung aller theoretischen Fragen übertragen. Auch die zugehörigen Flugversuche und die Höhenprüfstandserprobung des Turbinen-Luftstrahl-Triebwerkes hat Herr Decher geleitet. Im Jahre 1944 wurde ihm die Führung der Abteilung Vorentwicklung und die Vertretung des Hauptabteilungsleiters für die Entwicklung des Turbinen-Luftstrahl-Triebwerkes übertragen.

Dank seiner theoretischen und praktischen Begabung und seiner eingehenden Fachkenntnisse hat Herr Decher alle ihm übertragenen Aufgaben mit großem Erfolg gelöst und damit einen hervorragenden Beitrag insbesondere zur Entwicklung des TL-Triebwerkes geleistet.

Er hat sich durch größte Einsatzbereitschaft ausgezeichnet. Durch seine angenehmen Charaktereigenschaften erwarb er sich die Beliebtheit bei seinen Kollegen und Mitarbeitern und die Wertschätzung seiner Vorgesetzten.

Wir stellen Herrn Decher dieses Zwischenzeugnis auf seinen Wunsch mit Rücksicht auf die ungeklärten Verhältnisse in unserem Unternehmen nach Beendigung dieses Krieges aus.

JUNKERS FLUGZEUG- UND MOTORENWERKE A.-G.
MOTORENBAU STAMMWERK DESSAU

Reproductions of four Zeugnisse related to the letterheads

Prof.Dr.Ing. H. TRIEBNIGG
Chef de Département
Groupe Technique Voisin, Decize

Decize, 1-9-1950

ZEUGNIS

Herr Dipl.Ing. Siegfried D E C H E R, geboren am 2-11-1912 in Darmstadt, ist vom 1-12-1945 bis zum heutigen Tage als Leiter der Abteilung Regulierung im Rahmen der Vorentwicklung tätig.

Als solchem obliegt ihm die richtunggebende und verantwortliche Leitung und Durchführung aller Arbeiten und Versuche, die die Regulierung von Gasturbinentriebwerken im Rahmen der Entwicklungsarbeiten der Gruppe betreffen. Insbesondere geht auf ihn die Entwicklung eines neuartigen Regelsystems für TL-Triebwerke mit Verstellschubdüse und automatischer Regelung der Triebwerksdrehzahl und der Gastemperatur zurück, das unter seiner Leitung und seinem persönlichen Einsatz für das ATAR 101 bis zur Betriebsreife gebracht wurde. Dazu kommen unter anderem Auslegungsarbeiten eines Regulierungssystems für Turbopropulseure und Turboreacteure auf der Basis Zumessung der Kraftstoffmenge, Durchführung der thermodynamischen Berechnungen zur Auffindung der günstigsten Regelbedingungen für Gasturbinentriebwerke auf Grund von Messungen am Motor usw.

Herr Decher ist ein ausgezeichneter Ingenieur, der neben gründlichen technisch-wissenschaftlichen Kenntnissen über eine grosse technische Erfahrung auf dem Gebiete der Verbrennungsmotoren und Gasturbinentriebwerke verfügt und sein Aufgabengebiet der Regulierung souverain beherrscht. Er ist so eine der Hauptstützen unserer Gruppe.

Es ist anlässlich meines Ausscheidens aus der Gruppe und meiner Rückkehr zur Technischen Universität Berlin eine gern geübte Dankesschuld, dass ich ihm für eine mehr als vier Jahre dauernde vorzügliche Zusammenarbeit dieses Zeugnis ausstelle. Für seine Zukunft wünsche ich ihm besten Erfolg.

SOCIÉTÉ NATIONALE D'ETUDE ET DE CONSTRUCTION DE MOTEURS D'AVIATION

AU CAPITAL DE 5 489 400 000 FRANCS

SIÈGE SOCIAL : 150, BOULEVARD HAUSSMANN PARIS-VIIIe
REG. DU COM. SEINE N° 176.707 – RÉPERTOIRE DES PRODUCTEURS N° 8156 SEINE C. A. O.

BOITE POSTALE : 293 PARIS-VIII

COMPTE CHÈQUES POSTAUX : PARIS 1684-39

TÉLÉGRAMME : MOTAVIA-PARIS
CODE : BENTLEY II

Groupe Technique Turbo-machines
105, Rte Nationale DECIZE/Nièvre

LE 27-11-1952

IMPORTANT
ADRESSER LA CORRESPONDANCE IMPERSONNELLEMENT A
S. N. E. C. M. A.
BOITE POSTALE 293
PARIS VIIIe
EN RAPPELANT NOTRE REFERENCE

TÉL. CAR. 33-94 POSTE N°

V/LETTRE DU | V/RÉFÉRENCE | N/RÉFÉRENCE

Objet

C E R T I F I C A T

Monsieur Siegfried D e c h e r, Dipl.Ing., né le 2-11-1912 à Darmstadt, est entré en janvier 1946 comme chef de service aux Ateliers Aéronautiques de Rickenbach à Lindau-Rickenbach, société dont nous avons pris la succession juridique. En Juillet 1946 il fut transféré avec ses bureaux en France où il a travaillé jusqu'à ce jour comme chef du service "Régulation" de notre Département Avant-projets de Turbo-machines.

Monsieur Decher était responsable de tous les projets de systèmes de régulation de turbo-machines, de leur conception et de leur calcul du point de vue thermodynamique, de même que des essais de tous les appareils de régulation au laboratoire et sur le moteur. Il effectua l'étude des régulateurs en étroite collaboration avec le bureau d'études. En outre il était chargé de suivre toutes les difficultés survenues en fonctionnement et en cours de fabrication et de les éliminer. Par ailleurs, il a traité avec les fournisseurs.

Pièces Jointes

../..

S. N. E. C. M. A.

IMÉCO-ISSY

../..

Sur le domaine de la régulation, Monsieur Decher a suivi des voies nouvelles qui après le temps nécessaire au développement ont donné lieu à une réussite complète. Les nouvelles exigences qui se sont posées au cours du développement du moteur ont toujours été résolues par lui d'une manière satisfaisante au point de vue régulation. Plusieurs de ses propositions ont pu faire l'objet de brevets d'invention.

Monsieur Decher a fait ses preuves en tant qu'ingénieur, possédant d'excellentes connaissances tant sur le plan théorique que sur le plan pratique. Il était toujours très consciencieux dans ses travaux. En outre, il a su éveiller chez ses collaborateurs l'intérêt et la conscience professionnelle. A tout moment il a donné entière satisfaction.

Ses relations avec ses supérieurs et ses collègues furent exemplaires, et il sût toujours entretenir une bonne collaboration avec tous les services.

Monsieur Decher nous quitte de son propre gré, libre de tout engagement, pour entreprendre un nouveau travail. Nous regrettons vivement son départ. Nos meilleurs voeux l'accompagnent.

Le Directeur du Groupe Turbomachines

H Oestrich

Zeugnis

Herr Siegfried Decher, geb. am 2.Nov.1912, trat am 1.Dez.1952 als Leiter unserer Vorentwicklung in unsere Dienste.

Auf Grund seines umfangreichen Wissens und seiner Vielseitigkeit war es uns möglich, Herrn Decher für die verschiedensten Aufgaben auf dem thermischen und gasdynamischen Gebiet einzusetzen. Insbesondere hat er sich neben vielen anderen Aufgaben mit der Berechnung und Untersuchung von Auspuffschwingungen unserer Zweitaktmotoren für Fahrzeuge und stationäre Zwecke beschäftigt. Seine Aufgaben hat Herr Decher in überraschend kurzer Zeit mit sehr viel Verständnis und einem großen technischen Überblick gelöst.

Ferner hat er für unsere neuen Stationärmotoren die Kühlluft-Gebläse berechnet, Untersuchungen an unseren luftgekühlten Motoren durchgeführt und hierzu Berechnungsunterlagen erstellt, die grundsätzliche Bedeutung für die Entwicklung unserer luftgekühlten Zweitaktmotoren erlangt haben.

Des weiteren hat er sich mit sehr großem Erfolg als Begutachter uns zur Verfügung gestellter Fremdmotoren, die er auf Leistung, Verbrauch und thermisches Verhalten untersucht hat, bestätigt.

Es würde im Rahmen dieses Zeugnisses zu weit führen, alle die Aufgaben zu erwähnen, die er mit großem Verständnis und einem umfassenden wissenschaftlichen Können bearbeitet und untersucht hat.

Seine Leistungen, sein Können und seine praktischen Erfahrungen auf allen Gebieten der Gasdynamik stehen weit über dem Durchschnitt. Obwohl Herr Decher nur eine verhältnismäßig kurze Zeit bei uns tätig war, hat er sich bei der Vielseitigkeit der bei uns vorliegenden Aufgaben rasch und schnell in die Materie eingearbeitet und sich überall da, wo er Untersuchungen und Berechnungen angestellt oder Gebläse - insbesondere Axial- und Radialgebläse - ausgelegt hat, mit bestem Erfolg betätigt. Wir verlieren in ihm einen unserer wertvollsten Mitarbeiter.

Herr Decher verläßt uns auf eigenen Wunsch, um nach den Vereinigten Staaten auszuwandern. Wir wünschen ihm für seine Zukunft alles Gute und viel Erfolg.

J L O W E R K E
G.m.b.H.

Pinneberg, d.15.Jan.1954

APPENDIX 3
Refugee Floods, Loss, and Redemption

It is hard to appreciate details within a large event such as war. The suffering of ordinary people has to be told at a personal level. At that level, the role of leaders is irrelevant. War does not discriminate when it comes to who should be a victim of its violence.

The story in the following pages is a very small one experienced by people who, involuntarily, participated in the refugee flood from Russia and Poland at the end of World War II and the events that preceded it. It is told by one who went through the first phase of the flood: escape from the oncoming Soviet army. The raconteur is the mother of a very close friend, a man named Thomas Wuttke who entrusted me with this story. I got to know him because he married a young woman the author's family sponsored for a year-long visit to the United States during her high school years in the mid 1980s. We consider her an "adopted" daughter and I feel that I am Thomas's big brother. With my encouragement, he wanted to share this story because it paints vividly his mother's experience in the winter of 1945, and the time thereafter. It is a unique story and a common one like those experienced by many others, including untold numbers of whom did not survive and were consequently silenced by events. At the conclusion of the story, a few comments will be provided to paint a picture of the second refugee flood: the expulsion of Germans from the East.

The words that follow are hers. They were initially penned for a radio program by the South German Broadcasting (radio) organization. The program was to remember the stories of World War II as sufficient time had elapsed to allow the memories, bitter as they might be, to be recorded for posterity. Not everyone can tell a story like this for it takes a lot of healing to have taken place, healing that cannot be realized and strength that cannot be mustered by all burdened by memories of difficult, hellish experiences.

The author and subject is Elsbeth Müller. She married after the war, bore, and raised Thomas with her husband. Thomas's father was in the Wehrmacht and it is fair to say that his wounds, although psychological, were best handled with silence. That approach to living life after war experiences was, and always is, a common one.

In 1976, Elsbeth was asked to read a half hour story about her memories. This was a big new event for her. To prepare, she wrote out, probably many times, the words she was going to use. They were in German and tailored for an oral presentation. She was sixty at the time when Thomas was eighteen. He remembers the commotion around her radio appearance and saved the typed pages that are the basis for this record. Thomas asked me to translate the story into English so that the future generations have something substantive to read and to share that story with our English-speaking progeny. I think it powerful enough to be representative of what many went through. The words are an accurate translation modified only slightly to better suit the written word. In the section that are her words, the historical context is added in *italics.*

The historical and geographic background is important. East Prussia was a province in eastern Germany until the end of World War II. The region was overrun by the Soviet army as they moved west toward Berlin in the last months of the war. The flight of Germans was initiated by the advance of Soviet troops preceded by terrifying rumors. There was revenge in the air.

The Words of Elsbeth Müller

An event from a 60-year-old's life: One memory, of which there are so many

Sixty years. That sounds so long and yet is so brief. Much remains in my memory: both the good and the bad. One event is so strong that it feels like it happened yesterday.

The 26th of January 1945 was an unforgettable day. The memory cannot be extinguished. It was my war experience and completely changed my life. The Russians were here (*in East Prussia*)! It was a cold January day: minus 32 degrees. The snow was knee-deep made harsh by a cold northeast wind. It was a real East Prussian winter day. We awaited still the final victory (*in propaganda terms, the Endsieg*) and hoped for a good ending of this war.

In spite of the weather and with much deliberation, our family decided that day to join the great flood of refugees that streamed, uninterrupted, from East to West. The decision was not easy. We kept alive the hope to be able to return soon to the home we loved. One of the options available, but not exercised earlier, was evacuation by sea that would have involved travel to the Baltic. We had packed four large "Leiterwagen" to the fullest (*a small wagon with two ladder-like sides and a pull bar*). We wanted to leave nothing behind: dishes, clothing, etc. Everything was very carefully packed. I was a young woman (*29*) and engaged to be married. The stuff packed included what was to be my dowry and that of my younger sister (14), for a time in a later future. That this departure was to be forever was not taken to heart. We were always full of hope. It would, however, be forever. A goodbye to our "Heimat."

Our (*very*) small village was Wangen (*located in the Russian Federation today*), not far from Königsberg in East Prussia (*a German city since 1255 on the Baltic, now Kaliningrad in Russia*). My parents ran a small Hof and a Gastwirtschaft (*a small restaurant for locals*). It was plain with well-scrubbed tables. The Stammkunden (*the regulars*) were farmers from nearby. Kornschnaps, beer, Speck (*smoked ham*), meats, and wurst were available in abundance. We were never hungry, even during the times with food ration cards. *The word "Hof" is not translatable with all its nuance. It is a farm enterprise centered on an area surrounded by residence buildings, barns, stables, sheds, etc. with the adjoining fields further out. Often there are associated retail activities like a restaurant, a pub, or direct produce or dairy sales. In general, such a building complex may be enclosed by walls in which case the Hof is entered by a large, usually open, gate.*

In these surroundings, I lived out my youth. In all, I had wonderful years of growing up. My favorite pastimes included riding. No casual trotting for me, I preferred a faster ride. At sunrise, our horses were brought in from the pastures without bridles, reins, and saddle at full gallop. The paddocks were far away and it was always a joyful ride. East Prussia was a level land where one could see far—all the way to the line where land and sky met. Yes, Papa often scolded us because we rode too fast and the horses came in steaming with sweat. They would soon be hooked to field implements to go to work: plowing, seeding, and harvesting. All the work was done without the use of modern power machines. We also had 30 cows that had to be cared for and milked—also without milking machines. The chores were plentiful for my two brothers, my younger sister, and me.

The snack breaks in the fields were joyful times. I remember devouring the thick bread and butter sandwiches from the large basket in the shade of the big oak tree at the field's edge. We noticed nothing of inflation, unemployment, and want that plagued Germany in the 1920s. Stress and nerve disorders were foreign words to us. 1933 and the Hitler time were, for us, without great significance. We loved our land and we were happy. I was waiting to be married. My future husband also owned a small farm (*a Hof*) and that dimension was an important aspect to our planned marriage.

1936. Mandatory military service (*Wehrpflicht*) was an important milestone along the passage of time. My brothers left the farm and we had to do without them. My memory of the time was dominated by the presence of soldiers. They were everywhere. After maneuvers, they were always found in the local watering holes and at dances in the village. Music was supplied by home-made instruments like a Teufelsgeige (*a sort of violin made from tin cans and wire*), harmonicas, and when necessary, even combs to make a kazoo.

Real soldiers were an inspiration for us. We believed in the future and did not suspect that anything bad that might be coming. I saw that my parents were often sad and upset, but I could not and would not understand their concerns. I was young with nothing was more important on my mind than happiness and love. We were full of optimism.

1939. War begins. Even that reality was not a reason for panic or great concern. We were far from the shooting and it was projected to end in short order. Then came the invasion of Russia (*June 1941*). My father was conscripted into the Volksturm. Those were the people who were not usable for the army, irreconcilable with it, sick, or too old. I don't remember that time very well, but I believe that (splinter) trenches had to be dug, presumably to delay Russian military movements because, by that time, we had already heard of German retreats from the Ostfront.

September 1941. My younger brother serving in the communication service was killed. The house became much quieter and my mother cried a lot. I did not want to understand her reaction. Did he not die for the Führer and the Fatherland? We, the young, believed in that then. Today, I feel differently. Our little tavern became very quiet. The men were all gone, and mother continued to serve the few locals who came. In time, we received assignment of a French PoW (*prisoner of war*) who helped out with the farm chores. He was very nice and helpful around the farm. His name was Gabriel. He, my little sister, the elderly parents, and I held the place together. There was much to do and not much time for reflection.

(*Winter 1943*) We still believed in a final German victory. We sent packages to the troops at the front, baked Kuchen and sang joyous songs for the wounded in the nearby field hospital. The numbers of wounded kept climbing as the big retreat had begun. Countless deserters and wounded drifted in from the East. We tried to take care of them as best we could. One could say there was not a single family that did not have relatives to mourn but people held their miseries closely. We continued our work, never giving up and kept hoping for the Endsieg. Enemy airplanes dropped bombs, day and night. Königsberg and many other cities were destroyed under the hail of these bombs. We learned that the Russians had marched into Memmelland (*a part of Lithuania on the Baltic*). Soon thereafter, our house and barns were overrun with retreating soldiers, many, many of which I saw die. Then came the civilians, a truly sad train of folks.

The Russian troops were about 50 km from Wangen when the village became a military bridgehead or strongpoint for holding back the enemy. This is when we decided to join the refugees and leave to move west. It was too late.

26 of January 1945, 1 o'clock in the predawn morning. Along a forest path, we heard and saw Russian tanks move. They came like ants. Were there 10, 20, or hundreds? It did not matter. In a very short time, our

entire farm, courtyard, garden, fields, etc., was overrun by the tanks. Fences, trees, and everything else that stood in the way was leveled. Tanks and soldiers everywhere and, frozen in place, we feared for our lives. The soldiers went directly to our packed Leiterwagen, unpacked them, and threw everything to the ground. The wedding dress saved for my sister was paraded and danced around by a soldier who laughed and laughed. We did not know that most of the nearby villages were still controlled by German troops. At 6 am, the shooting started, to and from all sides. We sought shelter in the cellar together with other strangers. We shared terrifying minutes lying on the cold floor, hoping…

At the end of the noise, we were pulled out of the cellar by the Russian troops and forced to shelter in one of the nearby trenches. We could watch as all the buildings of our farm went up in flames. Horses, cows, pigs, poultry ran wildly about, many on fire. Whatever survived this horror was shot by the Russian soldiers. In a short time, it was all rubble and ashes. Three generations labored here and there was nothing left. A horrid sight of this destruction awaited us as we were pulled out of the ditch. There were Russian soldiers everywhere and smoking tanks in the smoldering rubble that was our beautiful farm.

We were brought to a neighboring house that survived the fighting. We got something to eat and regained a bit of hope that the worst was behind us. Not so. My 14-year-old sister was raped by a dozen soldiers on front of her parents. "Papa, Papa, please help me!" she cried. To no avail, they just laughed at us. I … (*words fail*)

It was a cruel and painful time for all of us. After a time, we and all other fellow sufferers were rounded up for a long march to the East, into the unknown. With only the clothes on our backs, toward a frozen horizon, we went with snow blowing into our faces.

We went on and on. The train of misery grew steadily as many others were added to it. The villages we encountered were burned out and empty. We were empty. Armed guards were all around us, at the front, along the sides of our parade of marchers, and at the rear, pushing the herd along. Their machine gun safeties were off, of course, ready to shoot. There was nothing to eat. Those who could not go on laid down and stayed put. A swift kick would roll the victim into the ditch on the side of the road and that was that. My mother shared that fate. She could not and would not go on. I fell on my knees beside her and wanted to die with her. A guard came up threatened me with the gun and I had to get back into the line of marchers. My mother stayed in the ditch and was soon covered with snow. That was the last time I saw or heard from her. Many, many others shared her fate.

We, the leftovers, kept going eastward, mindlessly, without hope, mute like animals. Nothing to eat. Occasionally, a frozen potato was found and enjoyed as a delicacy. Evenings, the column halted, sometimes in the vicinity of empty barns or houses. Here was protection from the hordes who were always seeking out women and shelter from the bitter cold. Occasionally we would find remainders of provisions for German soldiers, cans of rations or packages of dry soups to be mixed with water. These became celebratory meals. Even the grains in farm storage would be used for food. These were abundant as the winter provisions were plentiful. Wheat or rye, it did not matter, we ate it even though its original purpose was to feed the animals. Raw red beets and sugar beets also served as approximation to food.

I could understand the women who gave themselves to the Russians. I am sure that they did not do it for pleasure but to help the children and themselves to survive. They got bread and sugar for their submission. They did what they had to do. To survive, one also had to be able to negotiate with Russians in their own language. I learned quite a bit of it before it was all over.

Just before the Lithuanian border, my father was separated from the group. All the men were herded onto trucks. I finally broke down and cried. At mother's death, I simply endured it, much like a stone would. This time, I cried and cried without restraint. I did not want to go on. "Why you cry?" a Russian officer asked. "Your Hitler and your house soon kaput, your father go back home and you too, then all is good!" Well, nothing was good. I never saw my father again. Much later, I learned that he was transported to Siberia and died there. Our march continued eastward through Lithuania and into Russia. How far into Russia, I do not know, and I did not care. A muted herd we were and nothing else.

Then came the 6th of May 1945. We were overnighting at an abandoned farm in ruin. It was not difficult to learn that the war was over. The victorious Russians celebrated with fireworks and night long festivities involving Vodka and Schnapps that wasn't just drunk but poured over one another. There were immense amounts of food from somewhere. Whoever was hording it, no longer had to. It was all... for only the Russians!

Against the sky, a large placard with letters spelling out "Hitler and Haus Kaput" illuminated with fire, numerous times relit. All hell broke loose and yet it was just fireworks and pistol shots into the air. Amazingly, we were told that we were free. We could go wherever we wanted. But nobody spoke of "Where to?" We had nothing to eat, no prospects for eating. We were completely exhausted, had no means to do anything, but suddenly felt freed like a released wild animal running across the meadow.

The herd of people freed had been substantially diminished in number by a deadly attrition. It was time to think and we dared to plan. Fourteen of us women got together to plan for a return to our homes. My sister and I vowed to stay together. The group set off on a march again, this time westward and without guards. It was May. We collected courage and hope. We knew, however, what to expect when we got there, but that was unimportant right then. What was important is that we survived this long, and we have a chance to go home. That thought alone drove us to undertake our journey and endure the hardships to come.

We went through a dead landscape. Ruined and abandoned villages, savaged fields, burned out carcasses of cars, trucks, and tanks along the roads kept us company as a reminder of past violence. We ate meat from dead horses and cattle as long as it was marginally eatable. We hacked out the best past parts, washed them in the creeks, and roasted our meals over campfires of abundant wood. And it was summer.

A sad chapter of this journey was that, along our way, we buried many soldiers, German and Russian. Sometimes without any military insignia to identify them as one or another. We did this, our duty, as long as our strengths held up. We buried them without names without markers, sometimes 10–12 in one grave. It was not hard to find holes made by bombs and artillery shells as grave sites. Often, the dead were left more or less where they were and covered with fresh soil. Officially, they, whoever they were, would ultimately be listed as "lost" in the records of history.

By the end of summer, we made it home. We made it after four months of walking. The group grew smaller as individual women left to seek their villages. Should we have expected or hoped for anything wondrous and joyful? Not really, but we all did hope that perhaps that another member of the family also made it back alive. The village of Wangen was gone. Nothing left. Just tall weeds among the ruins. The Post Office was gone as was the town. It was a time to cry and to assess our very meager options.

Eventually my sister and I found that in the nearby estate of Hans-Herbert Brausewetter (The cousin of the screen actor by that name), the Russians had established a "collective." *This is a collection of people who were paid (in Russian Rubles) for contributing whatever they were able to do.* About 1,000 German PoWs and civilians worked there. I got a job in the cow barn to take care of 18 cows: feeding, cleaning, milking, and keeping the stalls clean. The calves also had to be taken care of. If or when any of these animals died, the talk was immediately of "sabotage." Those associated with serious events, fights, incompetence, and the like, were removed from the collective and never seen again.

The task of "guarding cows" was an awful strain. For this, four women had to keep watch over the giant herd of about 500–1,000 cows, animals collected from the farms in the area. Grazing areas were large. Many kilometers separated the healthy cows from the weakest as they spread out in the fields, my father's fields among them. All property had been confiscated and the fields no longer belonged to us. Many tears were shed, but what was the use of that? We wanted to live! When an animal died, someone was severely punished. When a human died, that was nothing. People who could not work, got nothing. We helped them as best we could. They would have starved.

My sister drove a tractor. She had to haul harvest wagons and do all the field work done with machinery. We had to work because we wanted to live.

We heard nothing from Germany. Was there even a Germany left? One could write a lot about this time, but it is hard to put worries and thoughts of uncertainty on paper. The time passed and we were paid. The meager amounts were determined by the number of liters of milk produced adjusted for fat content that was measured and evaluated. Everything was measured. We did earn enough to buy groceries. Clothing was supplied by the PoWs. They took old uniforms and repaired them. That kept them occupied. To the Russians, these clothing makers were specialists and that status carried with it certain advantages. Mechanics who could repair farm machinery, generators, etc. all were specialists; even those who specialized in changing light bulbs or fixing leaky water valves. There was a lot of trading going on. We divided loaves of bread and dealt in cigarettes made with Russian newsprint, *Pravda,* and the like.

We learned to understand the Russians, particularly that they were also human. My sister came down with typhoid fever and, to add to the misery, lice. She lost all the hair on her head and because of the lice, nearly the skin there. These beasts had nearly taken her down. One of the guards, named Nischa, whose duty it was to watch us, unselfishly took it upon himself to take care of her. He never demanded anything in return. He just gave what he could.

There were guards who had to keep watch on food stuffs and miscellaneous other material. They stood on guard and made sure that were not caught when things disappeared as we "organized" the stored material. A good memory I have is about a Russian officer who sang songs of the Volga region in German and in Russian. He had an unforgettable voice. His name was Dikma.

Deutscher Kriegsgefangener	*German war prisoner*
Ein grosses Dankeschön	*A great big Thank you,*
Du hast gut gearbeitet	*You worked hard*
Du kommst bald nach Hause	*You will go home soon.*

That was our motto, learned in Russian.

In October 1948, we were expelled. As suddenly as the Russians came into our lives, we had to leave them. It was time to say a final goodbye to our Heimat (home). Within a few hours we were loaded onto trucks and brought to Königsberg. Yet another journey into the unknown. We could not bring anything with us, but then again, we had nothing. We rode through Wangen one last time. The soldiers, whom we had befriended in our time together waved goodbyes. It was a nostalgic, complicated moment.

In Königsberg we were counted, registered, loaded onto cattle cars, and sealed in. There we were 48 persons, men and women, and straw on the floor. Nothing else. There were attempts at singing sad songs of goodbye to our country: "Nun ade du mein lieb Heimatland." It was very sad and soon the atmosphere descended to tears. We did not know where we were going and there was no one to ask. Sometime in November 1948 *(presumably after quite some time in the cattle car),* we arrived at our first station stop at Pasewalk (*just west of Stettin in eastern redrawn Germany*). There, we were thoroughly interrogated: where, why and how where you born? and endless questioning. After 14 days of quarantine in Pirna (*near Dresden*), deloused and examined, we were designated as human beings with official papers (*for the first time since 1945*). Then two weeks in Leipzig-Windorf. More questioning while living in a refugee camp. Finally, after 3 more weeks, my sister and I landed a place to live in a private room in Leipzig. The room was in the house of a very nice family with whom we shared a real Christmas, complete with presents!

I searched for family members using the auspices of the Red Cross and found my older brother residing in Karlsruhe (*in West Germany on the Rhine*). After Christmas we left Leipzig by walking 200 km to Eisenach (*on the east side of the border*). Near there, we illegally crossed over the new intra-German border on New Year's Day to join him. We had not known of the division of Germany and the existence of the heavily patrolled, but still unbuilt, border. The crossing was difficult, but we succeeded. Again, we were put into a refugee camp. More questions, after which we got new papers. After a couple of weeks, we landed in Karlsruhe and I got work through the Caritas Verband (*an old Catholic service organization*). The work was as domestic help but without access to housing. I had to provide my own. It was not easy transitioning from life in the East Prussian countryside to city life in Baden. First, I did not have much experience cooking, much less of the Badische Küche! The salary was good, however, and my savings grew. At last, I could see the beginning of something that resembled life.

In the years that followed I was always in the work force so that I am now entitled to a retirement check. I married and at age 42 gave life to my son, now 18. I am happy that, through it all, I managed. To end this story, I want to mention a saying that helped me greatly during those difficult years:

Take in every catastrophe as an event, but don't turn events into catastrophies.

Elsbeth Wuttke, 1976
(*nee* Müller, 1916–1997)
Rheinstetten-Forchheim

Thomas adds to this story that he is grateful and fortunate to have had such a resilient soul for a mother. His aunt who was with his mother on this journey was not as fortunate in life.

This story has a curious twist for Elsbeth and her sister. The Müller family had waited a long time to decide to join the stream of refugees. The family hoped for a reason to stay in the place they love. For a number of days, perhaps as much as two weeks, prior to the 26th of January, many of the residents had a chance to escape the Soviet army by sea by going to Gotenhafen (just north of Danzig, today Gdynia in Poland), a harbor on the Baltic coast near Königsberg. The *Wilhelm Gustloff* was scheduled to take refugees to Kiel.

The *Gustloff* was, before the war, a luxury ocean liner. Launched in 1937 and built for taking 1,463 well-to-do guests on cruises with a crew of 417. With breakout of war, she was transformed into a military hospital ship. With a length of 685 feet, she was a large ship.

Many refugees were taken on board during the last days of January. Official records indicate that almost 8,000 people were registered to be on board and estimates were that an additional 2,500 found their way aboard. There was much confusion on the ship's bridge with four captains arguing about when to leave, compounded by difficulties getting orders from the admiralty. When loading threatened to ground the ship where she was, it was time to move and they departed on January 30. After a 180 degree turn out of the harbor, she headed west. Sadly, at nine o'clock in the evening, with navigation lights on, three Soviet torpedoes found and sunk her. The four lifeboats with their capacity of about 100 each were quickly filled. She rests about 12 miles north of the coast and the site is noted today as a navigation hazard. More than 9,300 people perished with about 1,200 surviving. It remains the largest loss of life event by a single ship sinking in history.

Had the family of Elsbeth Müller acted more quickly to leave Wangen, she could possibly have been on that ship. Good friends of hers, then in Wangen and after the war, did get a spot on the ship and survived. War is chaotic. Luck, misfortune, and death are constant companions.

This is but one story of a difficult time.

The second postwar, refugee flood: historical context

After the war, the Allies redrew the German boundaries so that a large part of East Prussia went to a reconstituted Poland and some became part of the Soviet Union. The East Prussians were joined by many from other places.

Accepting and resettling these Germans in the West brought a lot of friction, shortages, and hardship to the Germans in the West during the postwar years. The assimilation had to be done by a new, sometimes not well-functioning, civil government and without much in the way of resources. The country was depleted of most of what was needed, primarily food and shelter. The bombing during the war had reduced housing in large cities to be almost nonexistent. Fortunately, the situation improved as time went on. The Western Allies, the Americans in particular, did play a solid part in helping alleviate the food crisis where they could. The abilities of Allied powers to help were hampered by their own states of physical and emotional depletion and by the reality that the defeated Germans were the enemy that started the war.

The numbers of refugees involved in the expulsion of Germany's eastern parts was large. The numbers are also hard to state precisely because there was so much chaos. When one talks about the population of Germany at a particular time, one has to consider that people who lived in annexed lands were counted. Thus, to start the counting, we have in 1939 about eighty million in the country. That includes annexed Austria and part of what later became the Czech Republic. The war brought death to four to five million German military personnel and to six million Jews in Germany and in occupied lands. Additional German civilian deaths range from half to two million, of which many were victims of war, bombing etc., genocide, and political exterminations.

The migration associated with the expulsion of Germans from the East, led to the divided Germany in 1950 having fifty-one million people in the West and a little less than twenty million in the East. Included in these numbers is the absorption of those expelled from the lands that were once German or where Germans resided. These numbers are estimated to be ten million who settled in the West and four million who stayed in what became the Soviet Occupation Zone and later the German Democratic Republic. Just like the Holy Roman Empire, as central Europe was called for centuries, and was neither "holy," nor "Roman," nor an empire, so was the GDR neither democratic, nor a republic. It was German, however.

These population numbers put the magnitude of the displacement into some sort of perspective. In the Western occupation zones about 20 percent of the residents were refugees from elsewhere. Illuminating is a view of population per square kilometer listed in census data that shows the resulting crowding in the West. On the Cold War front, it is interesting to note that the population in the West grew to eighty-five million in the early part of the twenty-first century while the population in the former GDR continuously decreased in that period, albeit modestly. No wonder the GDR felt the need to build a wall or iron curtain to keep people from leaving to a more prosperous and freer West.

As a German-American I am happy to be able to say that the uncertain postwar time was revolved quite decisively with the political realignments of the day that included the firm establishment of the Cold War. One of its first cold battles was the blockade of Berlin in 1948–49. Under the American leadership, the Western Allies made it clear that they were going to protect the Western German assets with the Berlin Airlift. The Western Germans now understood clearly what the Western, especially the American, role was going to be. The resulting very strong partnership between Germany with the West, even after Reunification, was a positive consequence for all concerned. It is not inappropriate to say that the creation of the European Union arose from these ashes.

BIBLIOGRAPHY

Decher, R. *Powering the World's Airliners.* Barnsley, UK: Pen & Sword, 2020.

Eggers, K. *Frankreichaufenthalt,* an unpublished life history, 2010.

Franz, A. *From Jets to Tanks: My Contribution to the Turbine Age.* Stratford, CT: AVCO-Lycoming, 1985.

von Gersdorff, K., and K. Grasmann. *Die Deutsche Luftfahrt: Flugmotoren und Strahltriebwerke.* Munich: Bernard & Graefe Verlag, 1981. In German.

Kay, A. L. *Turbojet History and Development, 1930–1960.* Vol. 1, *Great Britain and Germany.* Ramsbury, UK: Crowood, 2007.

Kay, A. L. *Turbojet History and Development, 1930–1960. Vol. 2, USSR, USA, Japan, France, Canada, Sweden, Switzerland, Italy, and Hungary.* Ramsbury, UK: Crowood, 2007.

Kay, A. L. *German Jet Engine and Gas Turbine Development, 1930–1945.* Shrewsbury, UK: Airlife, 2002.

Turner, P. St. J., and H. Nowarra. *Junkers.* An Aircraft Album 3. New York: Arco, 1971.

Walters, B. *Junkers: A Pioneer in Aviation.* Gloucestershire, UK: Chalford, 1997.

GLOSSARY

ATAR: (Atelier Aeronautique de Rickenbach) French organization of German engineers destined for relocation to France after the war

AVCO-Lycoming: Lycoming is the (gas turbine) engine division of AVCO Corporation

axial: Descriptive reference to an engine or compressor configuration wherein the flow is primarily parallel to the rotation axis of the engine shaft

BMW: Bayerische Motoren Werke, a German engine builder

bypass ratio: A measure of the amount of air processed by a fan relative to the amount processed by the core of a turbofan engine

compressor: A device for raising the pressure of a fluid

CV: French for "horsepower"; Cheval Vapeur (Steam horses). Used in connection with car models, it is a tax classification.

DDR: Deutsche Demokratische Republik (German Democratic Republic)

DM: Deutsche Mark, German currency between 1948 and 1999

fan: A propeller-like device for creating an air jet

Gruppe "O": Another name for individuals with reference to Hermann Oestrich; see ATAR

HQ: Headquarters

ICE: Internal combustion engine

ILO: German manufacturer of small engines

Lycoming T53 and T55: Turboshaft engines (see also AVCO-Lycoming)

Marshall Plan: The 1948 economic recovery plan for Germany

NATO: North Atlantic Treaty Organization, Cold War Western Alliance

Nazi: Abbreviation for "NSDAP"

nozzle: Device for converting a fluid at elevated pressure to a jet

NSDAP: Nationalsozialistische Deutsche Arbeiterpartei, German political party in power from 1933 to 45

Operation Paperclip: An American process for securing the services of German engineers and scientists after VE-day

pressure ratio: Measure of the output (relative to the input) pressure from a compressor

radial: Descriptive reference to a gas turbine engine wherein the flow is caused to flow in a radial direction

RLM: Reichsluftfahrtministerium, the German air ministry during World War II

RM: Reichsmark, German currency prior to 1948

Safran: Name of French aircraft engine builder after 2016, formerly SNECMA

SNECMA: Societé Nationale d'Etude et de Construction de Moteurs d'Aviation, National Society for the Study and Construction of Aviation Motors, now Safran

TH: Technische Hochschule, appellation for a German technical university

thermodynamics: A field of study concerning the nature of heat and power from engines, among others

thrust: The reactive propulsion force delivered to a vehicle by its engine

TL: Turbinen Luftstrahlantrieb, an early generalized reference to a jet engine in Germany

turbine: A rotating wheel with blades that extracts mechanical power from a jet

turboprop: A gas turbine engine fitted to drive a propeller

turboshaft: A gas turbine engine fitted to drive any kind of application

VE-Day: Victory in Europe after World War II, May 8, 1945

VEB: Volkseigener Betrieb, an East German (see DDR) state-owned company

INDEX

M

O

P

R

S

T